PASSING THE TRASH

A PARENT'S GUIDE TO COMBAT SEXUAL ABUSE/ HARASSMENT OF THEIR CHILDREN IN SCHOOL

Charles Hobson

Copyright © 2012 Charles Hobson

All rights reserved.

ISBN: 1478309121

ISBN 13: 9781478309123

Library of Congress Control Number: 2012913541

CreateSpace, North Charleston, SC

TABLE OF CONTENTS

Dedication v
Acknowledgements vii
Preface ix
A Parent's Perspective..................................... xi
Chapter 1   The Pandemic Incidence and Devastating
             Impact of Sexual Abuse/Harassment in Schools 1
Chapter 2   Serious Flaws in How Schools are Operated
             and Regulated 13
Chapter 3   Knowing the Enemy—Profiling Rogue Sexual
             Predators and Their Techniques 37
Chapter 4   Educators Who Enable, Aid, and Abet Criminal
             Child Sexual Abusers and Abandon Victims................. 51
Chapter 5   Advocating for Your Child—Know Your
             Legal Rights.. 57
Chapter 6   Filing Complaints 73
Chapter 7   Collecting Evidence to Prove Your Case 93
Chapter 8   Preparing and Protecting Your Child 103
Chapter 9   Surviving and Coping with the Trauma of
             Sexual Abuse/Harassment............................... 111
Chapter 10   Fixing Schools and What You Can Do to
             Fight Back.. 123
Appendix A   Selected References and Resources 161
Appendix B   School Sexual Abuse/Harassment Prevention
             Rating Scale.. 167
Appendix C   About the Author...................................... 183

DEDICATION

This book is dedicated to the millions of past and current victims of educator sexual abuse/harassment. I am sorry that our society, our educational system, and people you trusted have failed so miserably! I hope that the contents of this book will help you on your road to recovery, and empower parents to protect their children from ever having to endure this terrible trauma.

ACKNOWLEDGEMENTS

Many people made invaluable contributions in the process of writing this book. I would like to recognize and acknowledge their impact.

My wife, Rocio, for her strong unwavering support and advice.

My daughter, Natalie, for her research assistance, meticulous copy editing, and cover design work.

My daughter, Ana, for her research assistance and cover design work.

My son, Alex, for his cover design work.

My grandson, Sam, for his great drawing of the cover.

My brother, Bob (a Psy.D. clinical psychologist specializing in children and families) and his two colleagues (both Licensed Clinical Social Workers, LCSW's, specializing in children and families), Randy Hultberg and Rebecca Woodrow, for their advice concerning the treatment and recovery of child sexual abuse victims.

My brother, Randy, a retired middle school teacher, for his insights about educators and school operations.

Jana Szostek for her legal advice, selected copy editing, and strong moral support.

Jamie Connors for her research assistance, manuscript preparation skills, helpful comments on earlier drafts, eloquent Parent's Perspective, and strong moral support and encouragement.

Helen Harmon for her research assistance and moral support.

John Gibson for his insights about teachers and school operations.

Connie Milbourne for her advice on information dissemination and moral support.

Ranjan Kini for his advice on information dissemination strategies.

Subir Bandyopadhyay for his advice on information dissemination strategies.

My colleagues at Createspace, Niki Dawani, John Rieck, John Mark Schuster, and Project Team 5, who provided advice and support throughout the book publishing process.

Thanks to everyone.

Charlie

PREFACE

In January of 2012, I was doing background research for a second edition of my 2002 book about sexual harassment in higher education (The Lecherous University: What Every Student & Parent Should Know About the Epidemic of Sexual Harassment on Campus) when I encountered some deeply disturbing information that dramatically changed my thinking about sexual abuse/harassment in K-12. I had naively assumed that incidence rates of this problem would be low for two major reasons.

First, given that any sexual contact between a teacher and a young student would constitute a criminal offense, I assumed such sexual misconduct would be minimal. Second, since K-12 schools typically have close and direct control over students, I believed this would also reduce the likelihood of educator sexual misconduct.

Needless to say, I was stunned and outraged by findings in the following three reports:

1. a 2004 Department of Education report entitled, "Educator Sexual Misconduct: A Synthesis of Existing Literature", estimated that 9.6% or 4.5 million K-12 students are victimized by educator sexual abuse/harassment,
2. a 2001 report on a national survey of students by the American Association of University Women (AAUW) entitled, "Bullying, Teasing, and Sexual Harassment in School", found that 81% of students in grades 8-11 experienced sexual harassment at school and 38% responded that teachers (and other school employees) sexually harass students, and
3. a 2010 U.S. Government Accountability Office (GAO) report to Congress entitled, "K-12 Education: Selected Cases of Public and Private Schools That Hired or Retained Individuals with Histories of Sexual Misconduct", in which the Congressional Committee

> Chair George Miller (D-CA) found the biggest, most outrageous problem to be "passing the trash", a practice by schools of encouraging child sexual offenders to voluntarily resign in exchange for a positive letter of reference, no reporting to police, and no discipline.

I had no idea of the magnitude and severity of the K-12 sexual abuse/harassment problem, and had never heard of the unconscionable "passing the trash" practice. After talking with other parents, they have also been surprised and shocked by this information.

Thus, I decided to postpone work on the second edition book for higher education and instead concentrate on a book for parents (also grandparents) and concerned citizens about the pandemic of K-12 student sexual abuse/harassment.

Many people have already described the content of this book as too one-sided and too aggressive. I take these kinds of comments as compliments and make no apologies for my intentional and aggressive pro-student bias.

Innocent students have been brazenly victimized in silence for decades in this country, and powerful forces combine to produce the pandemic that we currently face. Effectively addressing the causes of this problem will require concerted and aggressive corrective actions. As parents, we need to more fully understand the dangers at school and work together to better protect our children. I hope the book helps in this effort.

All of the examples of sexual abuse/harassment in the book are real. I have set them apart from the rest of the text with italicized print. These examples come from two sources: (1) my own personal experiences with victims, parents, administrators, attorneys, and sexual predators and (2) published accounts of student sexual abuse/harassment.

I hope the book is informative for everyone who reads it and serves to motivate corrective action. Good luck, and let's work together to keep our children safe.

Charlie Hobson
July 2012

A PARENT'S PERSPECTIVE

When we find out that we are expecting, we begin to do all that we can to prepare for our child's safe birth. We take the vitamins and begin to read the books because somewhere, someone wrote their experiences down to let us know "what to expect". Then our bundle of joy arrives and we pack a bag full of everything but the kitchen sink and we continue to read the books so we keep up on "what to expect" during the first years. Then as she starts to grow we put her in swim lessons to teach her water safety. We teach her to look both ways for cars before crossing the street. We love her more than we ever knew possible. We want to keep her safe and give her the best start to life that we can. Unfortunately, sometimes those things are not fun. As a parent when you care about your child you do what you have to for her. This means letting her fall down while learning to ride a bicycle, taking her to the doctor to get her shots, and preparing her to recognize predators whose goal in life is to satisfy their demented desires. Did you just lose that warm, fuzzy feeling and feel the knot beginning to grow in your stomach? Me too.

My family and friends are all interested when I tell them that I am helping to research for a book that Professor Hobson is writing. Then once the topic is introduced they all get that uncomfortable look and then all of the excuses come as to why we shouldn't talk about "that". "Don't talk about 'that' in front of me; I don't want to think about 'that'. It upsets me." "'That' would never happen to my child because he knows about stranger danger." "Oh, I don't have to worry about 'that' because I live in a nice community where everyone knows everyone and that doesn't happen here." By 'that' do you mean sexual abuse/harassment on children in a school where my K-12 child is for seven hours or more a day, five days a week without me? I will tell you the same thing that I tell them. "I don't want to think about 'that' either. Some days the research was overwhelming and I would break down in tears but I want my daughter safe and the more I know the better chance I have of preventing this from ever happening to her." The look that I get then changes to concerned curiosity. Then the questions start. I share with them some stomach-churning statistics regarding teacher sexual abuse/harassment and a few of the heart-wrenching stories but then I tell them that the book will be out soon and that they really need to read it. <u>Passing the Trash – A Parent's Guide to Combat Sexual Abuse/ Harassment of Their Children in School</u> is one of the things that we as caring parents need to read to keep our kids safe. It is an unpleasant topic, but shying away from it won't keep it from happening.

Everyone knows about stranger danger, and no one would think twice about reporting if there was a child in the neighborhood that was being abused at home. A pedophile doesn't have a certain look. They aren't just the creepy man hanging around the park in a trench coat. They could be the sweet little old man that gives the best candy on Halloween or your child's third-grade teacher. What makes teachers so off limits? Some pedophiles think that they are very smart and they immerse themselves in a situation rich with their targets where they are the supervision. A school is the prime location for them. There are bad people everywhere and those few ruin it for the many who are there because they want to pass on their knowledge to the next generation.

Do not misunderstand me. I am not saying that all teachers are abusers. I love my daughter's teacher. I am saying that I want to cover all of the bases when it comes to protecting my children. I make no apologies for this. I would rather hurt someone's feelings because they don't understand me than to look into the eyes of my crying daughter and know that I didn't do enough.

People may think that I am too cautious or overly protective. I really don't care. As long as I answer to "Mommy" or "Mom", I will do whatever it takes to give her the tools to keep her from being prey for the warped and twisted walking among us.

Jamie Connors, mother to a preschool girl and stepmother to a fifth-grade boy

CHAPTER 1

THE PANDEMIC INCIDENCE AND DEVASTATING IMPACT OF SEXUAL ABUSE AND SEXUAL HARASSMENT IN SCHOOLS

"*Based on the assumption that the AAUW {American Association of University Women} surveys {of students in 1993 and 2001} accurately represent the experiences of all K-12 students, more than <u>4.5 million</u> {emphasis added} are subject to sexual misconduct by an employee {usually a teacher} of a school sometime between kindergarten and 12th grade.*"
U.S. Department of Education Report, Educator Sexual Misconduct: A Synthesis of Existing Literature (2004, p. 18).

Can you believe this stunning number? 4.5 million children are sexually abused at school from kindergarten through 12th grade, by school employees—typically teachers. Just imagine the human suffering that these young people and their families have had to endure! As a parent of school-age children, I was shocked, horrified, and enraged by this finding, when I first read it in early 2012.

Why wasn't this report widely publicized in 2004? Why weren't parents notified of this menacing threat to their children's welfare? Why didn't the Department of Education issue a national call for immediate, concerted action to stop this widespread sexual abuse of our children? Why didn't the President and Congress act?

I don't know the answers to these questions. All I know is that it is a national disgrace that we have knowingly allowed this horrible problem to continue in our schools without taking aggressive steps to stop it. As you read on, I think you will become as angry and outraged as I am, and demand corrective action now!

WHAT IS SEXUAL ABUSE AND SEXUAL HARASSMENT?

Perhaps the best definition of child sexual abuse is one offered by The National Child Traumatic Stress Network in their 2009 publication entitled, Child Sexual Abuse Fact Sheet: "Child sexual abuse is any interaction between a child and an adult (or another child) in which the child is used for the sexual stimulation of the perpetrator or an observer. Sexual abuse can include both touching and non-touching behaviors. Touching behaviors may involve touching of the vagina, penis, breast, or buttocks, oral-genital contact, or sexual intercourse. Non-touching behaviors can include voyeurism (trying to look at a child's naked body), exhibitionism, or exposing the child to pornography." It should be noted that these behaviors are considered criminal violations when the perpetrator is an adult, or being tried as an adult.

Sexual harassment is best defined by the Office for Civil Rights of the U.S. Department of Education, Revised Sexual Harassment Guidance (January 2001, P. 2): "Sexual harassment is unwelcome conduct of a sexual nature. Sexual harassment can include unwelcome sexual advances, requests for sexual favors, and other verbal, nonverbal, or physical conduct of a sexual nature. Sexual harassment of a student can deny or limit, on the basis of sex, the student's ability to participate in or to receive benefits, services, or opportunities in the school's program. Sexual harassment of students is, therefore, a form of sex discrimination prohibited by Title IX."

Pandemic Numbers of Sexual Harassment and Sexual Abuse Victims

The national professional society known as AAUW or the American Association of University Women has taken a lead role in studying the problem of sexual abuse/harassment in our schools. Their two most recent nationwide studies, in 2001 and 2011, provide the most accurate data we have about the incidence rates with students in kindergarten through 12th grade (K-12).

The AAUW 2001 report entitled, Hostile Hallways: Bullying, Teasing, and Sexual Harassment in School, found that 81% of the students surveyed in grades 8-11 had experienced some form of sexual harassment during their years in school. For the grades K-12, this translates into a mind-boggling number of 37,968,750 young people being victimized.

In a 2008 case in Illinois, the parents of a 12-year-old boy sued their son's school for failure to stop other boys from repeatedly hitting him in the scrotum, a practice they referred to as "sac stabbing". Multiple complaints by the parents did not result in any remedial action by the administration. The never-ending assaults eventually necessitated corrective surgery on the boy's testicles.

As noted at the beginning of the chapter, based upon the AAUW 2001 report findings, the Department of Education (2004) estimated that 9.6% of students in K-12 were victimized by educator sexual misconduct, for a total of 4.5 million. The 2001 AAUW report also documented that 38% of all respondents had witnessed teachers and other school employees sexually harassing students. This type of sexual abuse/harassment is especially damaging, given the positions of power and trust occupied by educators.

In an infamous case from 1997, a male school teacher/principal drugged an elementary school boy to make him incapable of resisting sexual advances, resulting in his death.

According to a series of L.A. Times stories in January and February 2012, former 30-year veteran South L.A. elementary school teacher, Mark Berndt, was charged with taking 390 photographs of 26 young school children, who were bound, gagged, and blindfolded, with large cockroaches crawling on their faces and mouths. DNA tests established that Berndt also spoon-fed his own sperm to the students.

The AAUW recently published a second report on sexual harassment entitled, "Crossing the Line: Sexual Harassment at School" (2011). A national online survey of 1,965 7th-12th graders revealed that 48% of them had been victimized by sexual harassment during the current school year.

If 48% of all students are harassed every single year in school, it is virtually assured that everyone will have been sexually harassed multiple times in the 13 years from kindergarten through 12th grade. Again, this is a national disgrace in desperate need of immediate and aggressive corrective action.

MOST LIKELY VICTIMS

Research provides us with reasonably detailed information about those students who are most likely to be victimized by sexual abuse/harassment. For example, the 2001 AAUW study found that girls are more likely to be harassed than boys, although the difference was small, 83% to 79%. A much larger gender difference was reported in the 2011 AAUW study of student-initiated sexual harassment, with 56% of girls being victimized versus 40% of boys. Young people whose appearance and behavior do not conform to traditional gender stereotypes also experience higher rates of sexual harassment.

The Department of Education report on educator sexual misconduct (2004) drew a number of disturbing conclusions about which students are most likely to be targeted. First, girls represent the majority of students victimized, 57.1%, to 42.9% for boys. Second, females of color are overrepresented as targets, compared to their percentage in the student population. Third, lack of appropriate educator supervision and oversight often places special education students at a higher risk for sexual abuse initiated by other students.

In a case against a substitute teacher in the Detroit Public Schools (2004), who allegedly told students to do whatever they wanted to as long as they didn't bother her, a young female special education student was forced to perform fellatio on four male students in the back of the classroom.

Clinical psychologist Stephen Rubin, writing in the book, <u>Teachers That [Who] Sexually Abuse Students</u> (1999), asserted that his research and clinical practice show that female students with the following characteristics are more likely to be victimized by teachers: (1) emotionally needy, often from dysfunctional, broken homes, (2) pubescent (going through puberty) or post-pubescent, ages 11-12 and up, (3) developmentally disabled, and (4) sexually precocious and adventurous.

Deadly Impact on Students

The list of damaging outcomes for students victimized by sexual abuse/harassment at school is frightening in its length and severity. Tragically, in extreme cases, young people may take their own lives!

In a case in New York (2009), a young female student was sexually assaulted by a male student in her computer class. Following the brutal assault, her grades dropped significantly, she was frequently absent, started psychotherapy, and was diagnosed with post-traumatic stress disorder and deemed a high-risk threat for suicide.

A 13-year-old male student in a California (2011) case suffered years of persistent sexual-orientation harassment from his peers. His teachers, assistant principal, and principal failed to take effective corrective action to protect him. Overwhelmed with the chronic torment, he committed suicide.

Sexual abuse/harassment has a clearly devastating impact on student victims. Combining information from the AAUW and Department of Education reports mentioned above, along with research data from The National Child Traumatic Stress Network, the effects of sexual abuse/harassment can be categorized in three main areas: Psychological, Physical/Medical, and Behavioral. Specific consequences in each area include:

Psychological

- lower self-esteem and self-confidence
- embarrassment and shame
- fear of attending school
- sexual confusion
- increased anxiety and stress
- re-experiencing the trauma while awake and/or asleep
- strong negative reactions to trauma reminders
- avoidance of trauma reminders
- post-traumatic stress disorder
- depression
- fear of being left alone

- increased nightmares
- decreased motivation and initiative
- suicidal thoughts

The 2001 AAUW national study found that nearly 1/3 of all students (32%) feared being sexually harassed at school, and almost half (44%) of all girls.

Physical/Medical

- impaired immune system functioning
- eating disorders
- sleeping disorders (insomnia)
- hyper arousal
- heightened startle response

Behavioral/Academic

- increased tardiness and absenteeism
- more conduct problems
- lower grades
- less class participation
- more changes of teachers and classes
- reduced involvement in extra-curricular activities
- more switching schools
- more likely to drop-out of school
- more anger outbursts
- age-inappropriate sexual language or touching
- indiscriminate sexual activity
- self-cutting/abuse
- suicide attempts

In general, the longer a child has to endure sexual abuse/harassment, the more numerous and serious the effects. Similarly, the more severe the sexual abuse/harassment, the more numerous and serious the consequences.

Sadly, the most crippling damage is done to those who are victimized by repeated sexual abuse over a long period of time.

The National Child Traumatic Stress Network, in an educational module entitled, "Understanding Trauma's Effects" (2010, p. 3-8 and 3-9), notes that chronic and/or serious sexual harassment, including sexual abuse, can have a crippling effect on a child's normal growth and development. They discuss key developmental tasks for school-aged children (6-12) and adolescents (13-21), and then pinpoint specifically how trauma impacts development for each group.

The disruptive effects on school-aged children (6-12) include:

- emotional swings
- learning problems
- specific anxieties and fears
- attention seeking
- regression to earlier behaviors

Trauma consequences for adolescents (13-21) include:

- difficulty imagining or planning for the future
- over- or under-estimating danger
- inappropriate aggression
- reckless and/or self-destructive behaviors.

I highly recommend The National Child Traumatic Stress Network (NCTSN) to any parent interested in understanding the impact that sexual abuse/harassment can have on their child. The information is research-based and presented in an easy-to-understand format. I will talk more about the resources available from NCTSN in Chapter 9, on surviving and coping as a victim.

The Department of Education (2004, p. 43) report noted some very disturbing long-term consequences for children victimized by educator sexual misconduct. The report asserted that, "For most children, being the victim of sexual misconduct does damage that lasts well into adulthood, and for most it is never fully repaired." Victims: (1) lose trust in adults and authority figures in general, (2) tend to drop out and stay out of school, (3) develop high rates of substance abuse, and (4) have life-long difficulties forming intimate relationships.

Stop Educator Sexual Abuse, Misconduct and Exploitation (S.E.S.A.M.E., at www.sesamenet.org) is a nonprofit agency dedicated to ridding our schools of sexual abuse/harassment. Their website offers first-person Survivor Stories, which are heartbreaking to read.

Two of the many stories recorded at the site include the following:

"I was 17 and he was old enough to have kids in their 20's. He was a teacher too and the chaperone for my high school ski club. He 'won' me on a bet race to the bottom of the run and when he asked me to meet him at the end of the session I said okay because that's what you do; you comply. I lied to my parents that I was going to the library and he raped me in the front seat of his car. I said yes because I couldn't stand to hear myself say no and hear him pleading any longer. I lost my virginity to a pedophile in the front seat of his car. We 'met' a few times after that and aside from the pleading and crying, the same thing happened. I wrote him off I guess when I left for college. Little did I know the problems were just starting."

"He made me feel special. I was 14, and didn't even like boys yet. Mr. L was the new vocal music teacher, a demanding, intimidating man who had a wife and a small child.

My mother wanted me to take piano lessons from him, which I did for one hour a week after school. He needed clerical help, and asked if I would do that after school in payment, so I stayed after school for an hour on a different day. The first time I sat at the typewriter, he stood behind me and put his hands on my shoulders. It was unusual, but I thought it was 'fatherly', and was flattered. When I took my piano lessons, he stood behind me, and often put his hands on my shoulders as I played. One day he reached down my blouse and fondled me. I stopped playing, totally shocked, and he took his hand away, talking about the music, and what notes I should have played – as if he were somehow not attached to his own hand. I didn't know what to do, so I didn't do anything. Sometimes he pushed up against my back. It felt disgusting, but I thought it was because I was special to him, and I was afraid of what he might do if I told him to stop. I also believed I must have done something to invite it, and felt ashamed.

One day he sat beside me on the piano bench, so I thought he would leave me alone, but he put his hand on my knee, then under my skirt. When I put my legs together, he stopped, but didn't say anything. I just gave in then. I knew what he was doing was really wrong, and yet there was some pleasure in being touched; so I felt even more shame. Sometimes the janitor would come in, so Mr. L would stop until he left. He molested me pretty much every week for the rest of the school year. If he saw me in the hall, he leered at me in a way that made me feel uncomfortable. At one point, I told him I needed to quit both the lessons and clerical help because I needed to study more, but he said it was too late to get a replacement for clerical help. He threatened to fail me in music, and I didn't think my parents would believe me if I told them the truth. Shortly before the school year ended, he told me to take inventory of all the music in the very small storage closet. He left, as he usually did while I worked, but this time, he went to lock the music room door and came back. He pushed me against the wall. He had never been rough before, and I knew I couldn't stop him from raping me."

Staggering Impact on Parents and Families

The National Child Traumatic Stress Network has explicitly recognized that when a young person is brutalized by sexual abuse/harassment at school, the devastating impact also affects parents and the entire family. The damage can be so profound and long lasting that parents feel compelled to sue the school system!

In an Arizona case (2009), a city police officer assigned to a school system sexually molested a 14-year-old male student on five separate occasions, severely traumatizing him. The family sued on behalf of their son, and on behalf of the parents, arguing that the police department's negligence and misconduct in training/supervising the officer caused the boy's parents to suffer emotional distress, injuries, medical expenses, and other damages.

In the tragic California suicide case (2011) discussed earlier, the mother's staggering grief led her to sue the school for the deprivation of her liberty interest in her son's companionship and society.

When confronted with information that your child has been sexually abused/harassed at school, any parent would be shocked and outraged. It is absolutely gut wrenching to see the trauma done to your daughter or son, and the suffering endured. Overwhelming feelings of anger, betrayal of trust in the school, revenge, and frustration can be completely paralyzing. For those parents who were themselves victimized as children by sexual abuse/harassment, your child's experience can re-trigger the earlier trauma you endured, making the current situation almost unbearable.

According to the National Child Traumatic Stress Network educational program, Resource Parent Workshop, Module 8, Taking Care of Yourself (2010), supporting and caring for a child victimized by sexual trauma can result in two problems for parents: Compassion fatigue and Secondary Traumatic Stress (STS).

Compassion fatigue can arise from long-term, intense caring and concern for your child. Common symptoms include: (1) emotional and physical exhaustion, (2) substance abuse, (3) over-eating, (4) disturbed sleep, (5) general emotional numbness, (6) decreased life and work satisfaction, (7) more mood swings, and (8) a wide variety of physical aches and pains.

Secondary Traumatic Stress (STS) is the trauma you experience as a result of your child's victimization and how she/he responds. Essentially, it is pain parents feel when their child is injured.

In spite of all of these feelings, it is essential that parents stay calm when first told about their child's sexual abuse/harassment and focus on comforting and supporting their child, and quickly getting her or him professional help. I will talk more about this topic in Chapter 9, on surviving and coping for victims and their families.

Treatment for the entire family is essential, as the stress associated with your child's victimization can impact everyone in profound ways. This can include strained relationships, increased dysfunctional behavior, and more episodes of abuse.

Suffering in Silence

While learning that your child has been victimized by sexual abuse/harassment is a parent's worst nightmare, the unfortunate reality is that the majority of young victims don't report what is happening to them, but rather suffer in silence. The 2004 Department of Education report (p. 34) found that: "Several studies estimate that only about 6 percent [emphasis added] of all children report sexual abuse by an adult to someone who can do something about it. The other 94 percent do not tell anyone or talk only to a friend (and they swear their friend to secrecy)." In The National Child Traumatic Stress Network document "What to Do If Your Child Discloses Sexual Abuse" (2009, p.1), they note that studies with adults who were sexually abused as children show that 2 out of 3 never told anyone about the abuse during childhood.

Results from the AAUW 2001 national study indicated that only 20% of sexual harassment victims reported the incident to their school and 24% to their parents or other family member. The 2011 AAUW study on student-initiated sexual harassment found that only 9% reported the incident to their school, with 27% sharing the information with their parent or other family member.

Major reasons given for the non-reporting include:

1. threats of harm if the victim told anyone,
2. doubts that anything would change,
3. fear of not being believed,
4. fear of being blamed for the incidents,
5. fear that the situation would get worse, and
6. personal shame or guilt.

Taken together, these function as powerful disincentives to report sexual harassment or sexual abuse to anyone.

This widespread reluctance to report should encourage all parents to keep lines of communication with their children open and actively utilized. Frank discussions about these issues before problems arise can reassure children that reporting is always the best way to respond to sexual abuse/harassment at school.

CONCLUSIONS

The suffering inflicted upon our children at school by sexual abusers/harassers is unbelievably widespread and devastating to victims and their families. This pandemic, out-of-control brutalization of young students is completely unacceptable and must be stopped at once. It is imperative that we provide a safe and secure environment in all of our schools. Anyone or anything that threatens student safety and welfare must be aggressively addressed!

CHAPTER 2

SERIOUS FLAWS IN HOW SCHOOLS ARE OPERATED AND REGULATED

According to Gallup's 2012, Confidence in Institutions poll results released on June 20, 2012, a record low was set for U.S. public schools. Only 29% of adults in the national sample expressed "a great deal" or "quite a lot" of confidence in public schools. This figure was down five percentage points from 2011 and represents the lowest number ever recorded, since polling began in 1973, when the value was 58%.

"In 2004, troubling surveys documented by the Department of Education estimated that millions of students are subjected to sexual misconduct by a school employee sometime between kindergarten and the twelfth grade (K-12). Interviews with actual offenders corroborate such statistics; one series of studies found that 232 {emphasis added} child molesters admitted to molesting a total of 17,000 {emphasis added} victims. In these cases, the individuals molested dozens, hundreds, and even thousands of victims, sometimes without ever being caught. In this context, you {Chairman George Miller of the U.S. House Committee on Education and Labor} asked us to explore how these individuals obtain and maintain contact with school children."

United States Government Accountability Office (GAO), Report to the Chairman, Committee on Education and Labor, House of Representatives, K-12 EDUCATION Selected Cases of Public and Private Schools That Hired or Retained Individuals with Histories of Sexual Misconduct (December 2010, p. 1-2).

How can something so horrible, affecting so many young people, happen in U.S. schools? Unfortunately, when the American public becomes aware of the information in this book, their confidence in schools will plunge even lower. Clearly, aggressive, large-scale corrective action is called for to address the huge problems present in our education system.

At a very fundamental level, if we can't provide children with a safe environment, free from sexual abuse/harassment, effective learning is impossible. Being fearful is not conducive to learning anything! Responsibility for the pandemic of sexual abuse/harassment in K-12 is shared among many groups and institutions. In this chapter, I will identify and discuss the most serious flaws in how schools are operated and regulated in eight major categories: (1) School Administrators and Administration, (2) Elected Officials and Applicable Laws, (3) Government Enforcement Agencies, (4) Teachers' Unions, (5) Collegiate Schools of Education, (6) School Accreditation Organizations, (7) State Teacher Certification Agencies, and (8) Teachers. I will close with a psychological analysis that helps explain why we have the pandemic in our schools. My hope is that by better understanding where the problems are, we will be able to develop more effective solutions (presented in Chapter 10).

MAJOR FLAWS

1. <u>School Administrators and Administration</u>

School Administrators

In this category, I include school board members and the superintendent. These people are directly responsible and accountable for how schools are operated. I should also note that we parents and other voters elect individuals to be school board members and they in turn hire and oversee the superintendent. Thus, if we are unhappy with how schools are operated, we need to take direct action to elect competent school board members and hold them accountable for hiring and overseeing a competent superintendent.

Perhaps nothing symbolizes the leadership failure of school administrators more than the phenomenon known as "passing the trash". This involves a secret deal between a school superintendent, teachers' union official, and a teacher who has been caught sexually abusing students, in which:

(1) neither the superintendent nor union officials comply with their legal responsibility to report suspected child sexual abuse to law enforcement or child protective services,
(2) parents are not notified that their child has been sexually abused,
(3) no attempt is made to provide counseling or other assistance to current and past child victims of the abuse,
(4) no discipline is taken or recorded in the abuser's personnel file,
(5) the superintendent provides a positive letter of reference to the next school, and
(6) the child sexual predator agrees to voluntarily resign.

Here is a sampling of what has been said about "passing the trash":

- *Chairman George Miller (D-CA) of the House Committee on Education and Labor, in response to a Government Accountability Office 2012 Report, K-12 Education: Selected Cases of Public and Private Schools that Hired or Retained Individuals with Histories of Sexual Misconduct (as reported by ABC News, December 15, 2010):* "But the biggest problem may be what Miller calls 'passing the trash'. These were cases GAO found in which school systems just let suspected sexual offenders resign, and even wrote them glowing letters of recommendation, so they could find teaching jobs elsewhere. 'My first reaction is just one of anger,' Miller said, "because I spent my entire life working with young children…and then to see that in fact with knowledge, school officials passed a convicted child abuser and molester on to another school system by covering up that information in the record. It's outrageous.'"
- *Education Week, December 9, 1998:* "Passing the Trash by School Districts Frees Sexual Predators to Hunt Again."
- *The Oregonian, February 17, 2008:* "They call it 'passing the trash', and it's a common policy that lets abusers resign and move to another district."

- *Department of Education, Educator Sexual Misconduct: A Synthesis of Existing Literature (2004, p. 44):* "Many school districts make confidential agreements with abusers, trading a positive recommendation for a resignation."
- *Teachers That {Who} Sexually Abuse Students (1999, p. 78):* "The rest of the case illustrates the 'pass the trash' syndrome which has existed for decades in school systems throughout the country."
- *Thompson's <u>Educator's Guide to Controlling Sexual Harassment</u>, June 2012, p.2:*

"Pennsylvania Bill Would Prevent Schools from 'Passing the Trash'". State Senator Anthony Williams has introduced a bill called 'Passing the Trash' that would stop school administrators from making secret deals with educators and child sexual abusers."

"Passing the trash" tells me a number of very negative things about the school administrators who negotiate and approve these deals. First, these "leaders" display utter disregard for the welfare of students—those who have already been victimized and those likely to be victimized at other schools in the future. Current victims are completely ignored and not offered therapeutic services to help recover from their trauma. In fact, no one represents the interests of children when these secret deals are made.

Second, these excuses for leaders send a powerful message that they are above the law and need not comply with their legal obligation to report suspected child abuse. This creates a climate of lawlessness throughout the school system and sets the example that legally required reporting is not necessary.

Third, these "leaders" display profound dishonesty. They provide a positive letter of reference for a known child sexual abuser without ever mentioning the misconduct. It is also dishonest not to tell the parents of abuse victims what happened to their children.

Fourth, these "leaders" exhibit a deep fear of teachers' unions and the potential lawsuits and workplace problems they can initiate. Although reporting to law enforcement and severe discipline (most likely termination) for the abuser are clearly called for, cowardice prevails and the wrath of the union is avoided by negotiating a "pass the trash" deal.

Fifth and finally, a single-minded focus on self-preservation is clearly evidenced, rather than any interest in the welfare of children. If abusers are secretly passed off to other schools, the "leader's" reputation and clean record are maintained, along with the public image of the school system.

I don't know how these people live with themselves, sleep at night, or rationalize their incredibly hurtful and damaging conduct. In my opinion, anyone who negotiated or approved a "passing the trash" deal should be incarcerated and banned from any contact with children. The damage that these school administrators have done and continue to do is beyond comprehension.

School Administration

To determine how effectively your school is being administered with respect to sexual abuse/ harassment, I recommend completing the rating scale attached as Appendix B. The scale consists of six major categories addressing important components of how schools should prevent and correct sexual abuse/harassment. The categories and associated points (out of a possible 100) include:

1. Formal School Policies (15 points)
2. Sexual Abuse/Harassment Training (10 points)
3. Student Support Services (5 points)
4. Complaint Processing and Investigations (20 points)
5. Discipline (25 points)
6. Public Reporting and Information Dissemination (25 points)

I will discuss major problems in each of these six categories.

<u>Formal School Policies</u> Specific problems with school policies related to sexual abuse/harassment include the following.

1. While most schools have a sexual abuse/harassment policy, they rarely include a zero-tolerance provision, indicating that all violations will result in some type of discipline, proportionate to the severity of the offense.
2. Schools rarely have policies prohibiting school employees from being alone with students.
3. Schools rarely have comprehensive policies concerning appropriate and inappropriate touching of students.

4. Schools have inadequate hiring policies that rarely require national, fingerprint-based criminal background checks or complete evaluation of prior work experience. These problems were prominently noted in the General Accountability Office (2010) report on the K-12 hiring and retention of individuals with sexual misconduct records. This report (p. 14) also noted problems with employees who committed sex crimes after being hired that were not detected by schools.

"This maintenance worker was convicted of misdemeanor sexual battery while employed by a California public school district. Since the district did not perform any recurring criminal history checks, district officials remained unaware of his conviction until we notified them. After this notification, district officials immediately confronted the offender, who resigned."

5. Schools do not have policies in place that expressly prohibit "passing the trash deals" and require honest, accurate, full-disclosure references for former employees.
6. Finally, schools do not have policies requiring annual student surveys on issues related to sexual abuse/harassment.

<u>Sexual Abuse/Harassment Training</u> I have had multiple conversations with senior school administrators about sexual abuse/harassment training for students and parents. In every instance, I have received the same disgusting response. Conducting training on this topic was completely out of the question, due to the expected increase in complaints. If you were in charge of a school, wouldn't you want to know if someone were sexually abusing/harassing your students?

Unfortunately, appropriate, school-based training is simply not being done. As noted in the 2004 Department of Education report on educator sexual abuse, when training is conducted for staff and students, teachers are rarely included as potential abusers. Training materials focus on other environments in which abuse can occur, but not schools.

When I do training for college students and professors on sexual harassment in higher education, the exclusive focus is on this environment and all of the examples involve scenarios from this environment. Failure to properly train school personnel and students is unforgivable. It allows teachers to prey more easily on uninformed, unprepared students.

I was unable to find any documentation of school efforts to effectively train parents about sexual abuse/harassment. Thus, I would conclude that schools have shown no interest in informing parents about how to protect their children from educator sexual abuse/harassment.

The near complete lack of appropriate training for children and parents is a major contributing factor to the pandemic of K-12 sexual abuse/harassment. Neither students nor parents have any clear idea about: (1) what their legal rights are, (2) what constitutes appropriate and inappropriate conduct, (3) how to protect students from sexual abuse/harassment, or (4) how to file a complaint. Sadly, until necessary school reforms are in place, parents will need to educate themselves and their children on these critically important issues.

Student Support Services The 2004 Department of Education report on educator sexual misconduct noted that: "The school or district rarely prescribes a therapeutic and healing intervention for targets of educator sexual misconduct...most school officials report that if action is taken against the abuser, they have done all that is necessary." (p. 45) Schools are oblivious to the trauma inflicted on child victims and fail miserably to provide the counseling and treatment necessary for recovery. As noted earlier in this chapter, "passing the trash deals" do not even acknowledge that victims exist. How shameful is this!

Complaint Processing and Investigations The 2004 Department of Education report on educator misconduct asserted that the majority of complaints are ignored or disbelieved, and this serves as a major deterrent to complaint filing. Commenting on the reluctance of schools to take complaints seriously and initiate investigations, the authors of Teachers That [Who] Sexually Abuse Students (p. 6) stated:

"Many administrators cling to the belief that one complaint is insufficient, two do not necessarily form a pattern and anonymous complaints should he discounted entirely. Faced with growing suspicions, some will convince themselves that only a written or in-person complaint is sufficient."

Given this dismal commentary, there are several specific problems with complaint filing and misconduct investigations. They include the following:

1. Schools rarely offer and publicize multiple complaint options, to include anonymous filing. This acts as a major deterrent to reporting.
2. When complaints are filed, schools do not make immediate counseling referrals for student victims.
3. Schools do a poor job in monitoring what happens to complainants to insure that no retaliation occurs, and taking corrective action as necessary.
4. Schools do not conduct some level of investigation for all complaints received, including anonymous ones. This discourages everyone from filing a complaint and allows the sexual abuse of children and all of their suffering to continue.
5. When schools do investigate complaints, it is often conducted by someone working for the district—either an administrator or legal counsel. How wrong is this? A credible investigation must be conducted by a professional outside the organization; in other words, an independent investigation.

According to the authors of <u>Educators That [Who] Sexually Abuse Students</u>, p. 158: "Any internal investigation of an agency by [the] agency itself is suspect." I couldn't agree more.

6. When evidence of criminal violations is uncovered in a school complaint investigation, this information is not consistently provided to law enforcement officials. The goal is to keep everything quiet so as not to tarnish the reputation of the school, its teachers, and its administrators. This is a big part of the problem with "passing the trash" deals.

<u>Discipline</u> The failure to discipline offenders is perhaps the most significant cause of K-12 student sexual abuse/harassment. Here are the specific problems in this area.

1. As discussed in the preceding section, teachers who sexually abuse students can rely on the fact that complaints about them will be ignored, disbelieved, and certainly not investigated. They count on enabling teacher colleagues not to report them. If caught, they can count on colluding union officials and school administrators not to

report anything to the police, but rather to negotiate a secret "passing the trash" deal that allows them to go to another school and continue their abuse. Without any criminal or disciplinary consequences, what is there to stop a pedophile teacher from sexually abusing children? How wrong is this?
2. Schools have not disciplined teachers for failing to report suspected child sexual abuse/harassment. How could they, when superintendents fail to report abuse in "passing the trash" deals?
3. The 2001 American Association of University Women (AAUW) report, "Hostile Hallways: Bullying, Teasing, and Sexual Harassment in Schools", found that 81% of surveyed students reported having been sexually harassed at school, most often by other students. The report also revealed that 38% of those responding had seen teachers and other employees harassing students. Finally, a 2011 report from the AAUW (p. 32) stated, "In several studies, students noted that even when sexual harassment happens right in front of teachers, few teachers do anything about it." Taken together, these findings suggest that student-on-student sexual harassment is widespread, ineffectively monitored, and rarely results in appropriate disciple. If kids see teachers "getting away with it" and no one seems to care, when student-on-student sexual harassment occurs, what is there to stop student abusers? This sorry state of affairs has got to change!

Public Reporting and Information Dissemination Schools go to great lengths to protect their reputation and conceal anything that might be damaging. A case in point is the "passing the trash deal", which is always secretly negotiated and concluded.

Schools are not legally required to release information to the public concerning: (1) annual sexual abuse/harassment incidence rates, (2) an annual summary of how sexual abuse/harassment cases were handled (without names), or (3) annual student surveys on sexual abuse/harassment, and thus they do not. This leaves everyone else (other than senior administrators) "in the dark" about the presence and magnitude of the sexual abuse/harassment problem in schools – just the way the administration likes it to be.

Schools don't want anyone to know how serious this problem is or even how/where to file a complaint. Ideally, incidence information should be easily available to all students, parents, and taxpayers/citizens.

<u>Tenure</u>   No consideration of problems in school administration would be complete without a discussion of tenure.

"For a teacher with tenure and a really strong union, you'd literally have to kill someone to be terminated." (quote from a former tenured high school teacher in a medium-sized Midwestern city).

Most states have tenure statutes that protect public school teachers from arbitrary dismissal. Typically, after a probationary period that can last from one to seven years, a teacher automatically receives tenure. In order to terminate a tenured teacher, a school district must show "just cause"; in other words, a valid, job-related reason for the termination.

While on the surface, this may seem to be a reasonable process, in actuality, teacher tenure, as vigorously supported by unions, has made it extremely difficult, time-consuming, and expensive to terminate teachers for sexual misconduct or any other reason. To illustrate the problems caused by teacher tenure, consider the following examples from the website teachertenure.procon.org, which offers facts and arguments both in favor of and against teacher tenure:

"Tenure makes it costly to remove a teacher with poor performance or who is guilty of wrongdoing. It costs an average of $250,000 to fire a teacher in New York City. New York spent an estimated $30 million a year paying tenured teachers accused of incompetence and wrongdoing to sit in 'rubber rooms', before those rooms were shut down on June 28, 2010."

"A Feb. 11, 2010 LA Weekly investigation found that Los Angeles Unified School District spent $3.5 million trying to fire seven underperforming teachers. On average, legal struggles to remove each teacher took five years and ended with four of the teachers being fired. Thirty-two other underperforming teachers were given an average of $50,000 by the district to quit."

"In 2000, Georgia Governor Roy Barnes, a Democrat, successfully pushed a law through the legislature eliminating tenure for new teachers. Barnes told a joint session of the General Assembly, 'Most of the time, tenure means a principal doesn't even try to dismiss a bad teacher because, even if the principal bucks the odds and succeeds, the cost in time and money is staggering.'"

"With job protections through court rulings, collective bargaining, and state and federal laws, teachers today no longer need tenure to protect them from dismissal. For this reason, few other professions offer tenure because employees are adequately protected with existing laws."

Teacher tenure is also one of the factors commonly cited as motivating school superintendents to negotiate "passing the trash" deals.

In my opinion, tenure systems for public school teachers are a major contributing cause of the student sexual abuse/harassment pandemic. As such, concerted action is needed to significantly modify or abolish them.

<u>Financial Accountability</u> Public schools are nonprofit organizations, funded primarily by taxpayers. In contrast to for-profit organizations, schools do not answer to stockholders/investors who demand cost-effective operations in order to maximize profit.

I contend that taxpayers have been "kept in the dark" by schools about the staggering financial costs associated with sexual abuse/harassment of students. Schools have hidden these costs and have not been held accountable by taxpayers. If taxpayers knew the full cost of sexual abuse/harassment in schools, they would not tolerate continued anemic efforts to control the problem.

Here is a listing of the kinds of costs incurred by schools found guilty of failing to prevent and/or correct the sexual abuse/harassment of students:

1. damage awards, although a percentage will be paid by the school's insurance firm (an article in the October 2005 issue of The School Administrator noted that Orange County, CA agreed to settle a sexual abuse case brought by six boys against their 4th-grade teacher for <u>$6.8 million</u>—at a time when school budgets were tight),
2. annual premiums for liability insurance for sexual abuse/harassment of students, which rise dramatically when damage awards are paid,
3. legal fees for outside attorneys representing the school in lawsuits, or the dollar value of the considerable time spent by school attorneys on such cases,
4. the dollar value of the time spent by school administrators and employees in responding to complaints and complying with court orders,
5. the cost of supplies and equipment used in responding to complaints, and
6. the cost of any expert witnesses used in the school's defense.

The total of these costs can be astronomical, yet taxpayers are not informed. Serious reforms are not initiated by schools because they are not being held accountable for misappropriation of public funds to pay for chronic mismanagement of the sexual abuse/harassment problem. Shareholders in for-profit companies would not tolerate this outrageous conduct and taxpayers should not either.

2. <u>Elected Officials and Laws</u>

The 2004 Department of Education report "Educator Sexual Misconduct: A Synthesis of Existing Literature", was prepared in response to a congressional mandate to conduct a national study of sexual abuse in U.S. schools. Similarly, the Government Accountability Office produced a 2010 report, K-12 Education – Selected Cases of Public and Private Schools that Hired or Retained Individuals with Histories of Sexual Misconduct, for the U.S. House of Representatives, Committee on Education and Labor. As noted earlier in this chapter, the chairman, Representative George Miller, described "passing the trash" as outrageous.

Unfortunately, in spite of these two damning reports, our national elected officials, President, Senators, and Representatives, have utterly failed to respond with corrective action to address this horrible problem. The complete lack of response is unimaginable, turning their backs on the 4.5 million estimated K-12 victims of educator sexual misconduct in the Department of Education report. No new initiatives have been implemented, no new legislation has been passed, no call to action has been issued – nothing, and the silence is deafening.

As I will discuss in more depth in Chapter 5, the federal laws protecting students from sexual abuse/harassment at school are anemic, and much weaker than those protecting employees from sexual harassment in the workplace! Additionally, Supreme Court decisions interpreting the primary law protecting students from sexual abuse/harassment (Title IX of the 1972 Education Amendments) have established standards of proof for student cases that are often impossible to attain. In her testimony to the U.S. Commission on Civil Rights (May 13, 2011), Fatima Goss-Graves (Vice President for Education and Employment at the National Women's Law Center) made the following comments about two major Supreme Court decisions (p. 7):

"That said, the effect of the Supreme Court's decisions in Gebser and Davis cannot be overstated. Simply put, these decisions have substantially hampered the ability of private litigants to receive full compensation under Title IX for their injuries resulting from past sexual harassment. Schools that ignore harassment can increasingly act with impunity."

Clearly, national action is needed by the President and Congress to address this pandemic. I will talk more about specific recommendations at both the federal and state levels in Chapter 10.

3. Government Enforcement Agencies

The federal agency responsible for protecting children from sexual abuse/harassment at school (K-12 and college) and responding to complaints is the Office for Civil Rights (OCR) of the Department of Education. I will discuss the OCR in more depth in Chapter 5.

Suffice it to say at this point that the OCR has failed miserably in its responsibility to protect students. After the damning 2004 Department of Education and 2010 Government Accountability Office reports (mentioned above), I would have expected a strong response from the OCR about how to address these national problems. Once again, the silence is deafening.

Congress has not provided the OCR with the necessary enforcement tools or budget to effectively address sexual abuse/harassment in schools. Unlike the Equal Employment Opportunity Commission (EEOC), which is responsible for workplace sexual harassment, the OCR cannot sue organizations on behalf of victims. Although the OCR officially has the power to recommend that federal funding be stopped for an offending school, this action has <u>never</u> been taken. Thus, the federal agency charged with protecting our children is essentially a "toothless, declawed tiger" with basically no enforcement power.

The irrelevance of the OCR in K-12 schools is reflected in the following, most recently available statistic. Of the total number of sexual abuse/harassment complaints filed by students in FY 2008 (69), none of them were from K-12. No one knows about the option to file a complaint with the OCR, and if they do, why bother, because the OCR has virtually no enforcement authority. This is unacceptable, from my perspective, and needs to be corrected.

Chapter 6 will discuss complaint filing options for victims of sexual abuse/harassment. If you suspect that criminal violations have occurred, a complaint should be filed with the police. Based upon a preliminary assessment of your complaint and supporting evidence, the prosecutor's office (city, county, state) will decide whether criminal charges will be filed against the alleged sexual abuser.

Two potential problems can arise at this point. First, if the prosecutor's office is severely under-funded and under-staffed, it may not have the resources to pursue your case. Second, in prioritizing cases to pursue, a prosecutor's office may conclude that allegations of sexual abuse against a teacher are not as serious as other pending cases, and thus not file criminal charges against the alleged abuser. In both of these situations, criminal charges that should be filed are not, further jeopardizing student safety and welfare.

4. Teachers' Unions

Teachers' unions provide blind, unquestioning support to child sexual abusers, masquerading as teachers, regardless of how heinous their crimes, and fully participate in negotiating "passing the trash deals" for offenders. The union "leaders" who negotiate these deals display the same glaring faults as do participating school administrators. This includes a complete disregard for the welfare of both current and future child victims of the abuser, utter contempt for the law and legal requirement to report suspected child abuse, dishonesty in failing to inform parents of the harm done to their children, and a single-minded pursuit of union goals at the expense of children's welfare.

The negative impact that unions have on the problem of educator sexual misconduct is illustrated in the following widely cited quote from the late Albert Shanker, President of the American Federation of Teachers union from 1974-1997:

"When school children start paying union dues, that's when I'll start representing the interests of school children."

Based upon my research on the role of unions in the pandemic incidence of K-12 student sexual abuse/harassment, I see the following specific problems: (1) opposition to any effort to discipline teachers for sexual abuse/harassment of students, (2) opposition to legally required reporting of child sexual abuse/harassment to law enforcement authorities, (3) opposition to more rigorous screening of applicants in the hiring process, (4) opposition to periodic screening of current employees for criminal offenses, (5) opposition to keeping disciplinary actions in an employee's permanent personnel file, (6) opposition to training teachers, students, and parents about educator sexual abuse/harassment, and (7) opposition to national and/or state legislation that would provide more protections for students. Finally, the 2004 Department of Education report on Educator Sexual Misconduct noted (p.46): "There is no research that documents teacher union attempts to identify predators among their members," and (p. 41): "National teacher associations [unions], to date, have not included suggestions for preventing educator sexual misconduct nor conducted studies of incidence."

As you can readily see, teachers' unions have a substantial, negative effect on the safety and welfare of school children, preferring instead to vigorously protect child sexual abusers/harassers masquerading as teachers. This threat to child wellbeing is very disgusting, in my opinion, and needs to be dealt with aggressively.

5. Collegiate Schools of Education

The teachers who sexually abuse/harass students, the enabling teachers who fail to report the sexual abuse/harassment, and the colluding administrators who fail to report the sexual abuse/harassment and negotiate "passing the trash" deals virtually all graduated from collegiate schools of education in the United States. These individuals were screened, admitted, trained, evaluated, and supervised in student teaching assignments. Thus, in my opinion, collegiate schools of education must share in the responsibility for the pandemic of student sexual abuse/harassment.

I wonder which university schools of education have the highest rates of graduates who are convicted of sex crimes with students, and which ones have the lowest rates? What are schools in these two groups doing differently? I have not seen evidence that collegiate schools of education have accepted any responsibility for the pandemic of student sexual abuse/harassment. Consequently, I have not seen any concerted efforts on the part of collegiate schools of education to meaningfully address this problem, through: (1) more careful screening and admission of students, (2) more effective training of students, or (3) more effective oversight and evaluation of individuals during their student teaching assignments. Clearly, collegiate schools of education need to accept their responsibility for the student sexual abuse/harassment problem and work aggressively to develop and implement solutions.

6. School Accreditation Organizations

The U.S. Department of Education recognizes six regional school accrediting agencies in the United States. These organizations are responsible for establishing standards for education quality and evaluating schools against these standards. As you might imagine, it is highly desirable for schools to obtain and maintain their regional accreditation.

The primary problem with this process is that the regional accrediting agencies do not specifically or comprehensively address issues related to the prevention and correction of student sexual abuse/harassment. Thus, there are no quality standards for schools to follow, like those contained in the school rating scale in Appendix B. Were such standards part of the accreditation evaluation, schools would be highly motivated to meet them.

7. State Certification of Teachers

All states have requirements that prospective teachers must meet in order to earn a teaching certificate, which is legally required in order to teach. There is significant variation in these requirements from state to state. Potential problems occur with this process in the following areas.

1. States do not consistently require fingerprint-based national criminal background checks, thus allowing convicted sexual predators to work as teachers in states other than those in which they were convicted.
2. States do not include "failure to report suspected child sexual abuse" as grounds for immediate revocation of one's teaching certificate. If this were the case, more teachers would step forward and report abuse.
3. State offices that oversee teacher certification are notoriously underfunded and under-staffed. This often means that processing revocation of certification cases is delayed and/or substantially lengthened.

During this time, sexual predators can continue to legally teach because their certification has not been revoked.

8. Teachers

In case after case after case of educator sexual abuse of students, the facts show that the crimes were committed over a long period of time and many teachers and administrators were aware of what was happening, but failed to report it. I'll talk in more depth about this topic in Chapter 4 (Educators Who Enable, Aid, and Abet Criminal Child Sexual Abusers and Abandon Victims).

If 4.5 million K-12 children are victims of educator misconduct, as asserted in the 2004 Department of Education report, odds are very high that many teachers have been aware of abuse/harassment occurring, but failed in their legal responsibility to report it. This failure persists, in spite of anonymous tip lines in many states for reports of child sexual abuse.

Teachers who fail to report sexual abusers ignore the trauma suffered by past, current, and future student victims. I fail to understand how this is possible for people who are supposed to have an interest in the welfare of children.

After publication of the 2004 report, there is no indication in the research I have done that teachers, collectively or individually, responded in any meaningful manner to the damning statistics. Thus, I am strongly inclined to support the following assertions made by the authors of Teachers that {Who} Sexually Abuse Students:

"When teachers deny knowing anything about longtime sexual abusers, it is often because they do not want to see or hear anything."

With respect to teacher-student sexual abuse, the entire K-12 school system is "not just an ostrich with its head in the sand, it is an ostrich which dons blinders and earplugs before putting its head in the sand." (p. 17)

Clearly, something needs to be done to energize teachers to take ownership of this national problem as a profession and do something about it. They need to get off the sidelines and get in the game, as their profession has "two black eyes".

PSYCHOLOGICAL ANALYSIS

A brief discussion about some important topics in basic psychology can be helpful in understanding why sexual abuse/harassment of K-12 students is so widespread and how to stop it.

In the history of psychology, behaviorists (most notably, Dr. B. F. Skinner) asserted that most, if not all of human behavior was determined by its consequences. In other words, if a particular behavior were followed by a significant reward, the likelihood of that behavior being repeated in the future is high. Similarly, if a behavior is followed by a potent punishment, it is not likely to be repeated again in the future. For example, a child who is praised for helping a classmate is more likely to help others again in the future or a child who is reprimanded for being late to class is more likely to be punctual in the future.

Cognitive psychologists (like Dr. Victor Vroom) expanded upon behaviorism and demonstrated that much of human behavior is a result of <u>expected</u> consequences. Thus, if a child expects to receive a significant reward for a certain behavior, she/he is likely to exhibit that behavior. In a similar manner, if a child expects to receive a strong punishment for a particular behavior, she/he is much less likely to exhibit that behavior.

For instance, if a third-grader is told that she/he will receive an extra 1/2-hour of recess if her/his work is completed, the student will typically strive to complete the work. Conversely, if a third-grader is told that she/he will be denied recess if talking during class occurs again, she/he is likely to remain quiet.

In order to modify and control human behaviors, cognitive psychology emphasizes the critical importance of clearly communicating the consequences or outcomes associated with behavior. If strong rewards and punishments can be explicitly linked with desirable and undesirable behaviors, one can exert a powerful influence on human behavior.

Workplace Applications

Dr. Louise Fitzgerald (the world's foremost expert on workplace sexual abuse/harassment, prominent researcher, victims' advocate, and expert witness) and her colleagues have conclusively shown that the number one cause of workplace sexual abuse/harassment is the absence of expected disciplinary consequences. Thus, if an organization does not discipline or punish managers/employees who sexually abuse/harass others, the incidence rates of abuse and harassment will be high. Why, because potential and actual abusers/harassers don't expect to be disciplined, if they get caught. On the other hand, if an organization adopts a "zero-tolerance policy" and disciplines (including termination for serious or repeated offenses) sexual abusers/harassers, the incidence of abuse and harassment will be low. I have seen this countless times in the organizations that I consult with and many court cases when I functioned as an expert witness. Oftentimes, employees don't take a company's anti-sexual abuse/harassment policy seriously, until they see that a high-level manager or long-term employee was in fact fired for violating the policy. Once this happens, the perceived expectation of termination, if caught, increases dramatically, thus significantly reducing the incidence of sexual abuse/harassment.

Applications to K-12

Let's talk about how all of this applies to the pandemic of sexual abuse/harassment in K-12. Based upon an analysis of this problem, my strong sense is that none of the key players expect any negative consequences or punishments for their actions that harm children. Specifically, here is how this works with: (1) teachers/educators who sexually abuse/harass children, (2) colluding school superintendents, (3) colluding union officials, and (4) other enabling teachers/educators who know about the abuse/harassment and do nothing.

Collusion: a secret agreement between 2 or more persons for a deceitful, fraudulent, or unlawful purpose.

Teachers/Educators who prey upon and sexually abuse/harass K-12 students have no or low expectations that their actions will result in:

1. someone filing a complaint with law enforcement,
2. someone filing a complaint with the school,
3. criminal charges and jail time,
4. civil lawsuits by parents of abused children for monetary damages,
5. disciplinary action by the school system,
6. negative references to future employers, or
7. loss of teaching license.

Without these punishments to worry about, sexual predators are free to gratify their perverse sexual desires and possibly repeatedly abuse/harass as many students as they can handle. The predators know that if caught, they will be able to work out a secret "passing the trash" deal with their union and school administration in which they will voluntarily resign, in exchange for:

(1) no reporting to the police,
(2) no disciplinary action taken,
(3) no indication in their personnel file about the incident, and
(4) a positive letter of reference for the next school they apply to.

<u>Colluding School Superintendents</u> who negotiate secret "passing the trash" deals with known sexual abusers/harassers of K-12 students have <u>no or low expectations</u> that their actions will result in:

1. someone filing a complaint with law enforcement against them personally,
2. someone filing a complaint with the school,
3. criminal charges and jail time,
4. civil lawsuits by parents of abused children for monetary damages, and
5. disciplinary action by the school system.

By concluding a secret "passing the trash" deal, colluding school superintendents are able to avoid any negative publicity and protect the "reputation" of the school system, as well as their own personal and professional "reputation". This conduct shows a brazen and criminal disregard for the welfare of children within their own school district and children in other school districts where the predator will be employed in the future. Unfortunately, since these "passing the trash" deals are negotiated secretly, no one, including victims and their parents, knows about what is happening. Thus, no one has the basis for filing a criminal or civil complaint against the superintendent, or a civil complaint against the school.

My only response to behavior like this from a superintendent is that it is unconscionable, unlawful, and should result in a prison sentence. These cowards, who are oblivious to child welfare and their legal reporting responsibilities, should never be allowed to work around children again. Ideally, with rigorous screening procedures, schools would never hire someone like this for the position of superintendent.

<u>Colluding Union Officials</u> who help negotiate secret "passing the trash" deals with the school system on behalf of sexual predators who are union members have <u>no or low expectations</u> that their actions will result in:

(1) someone filing a complaint with law enforcement against them personally,
(2) someone filing a complaint with the union,
(3) criminal charges and jail time, or
(4) civil lawsuits by parents of abused students for monetary damages.

Due to the secret nature of these "passing the trash" agreements, union officials are able to avoid any negative publicity and protect the "reputation" of the union as a strong defender of teachers, no matter what the offense or what crimes were committed. In such cases, when teachers, who are rumored to have engaged in serious misconduct, depart, without facing discipline and with a positive letter of reference, it is viewed as "proof-positive" of the unquestioning support of teachers by the union and its elected officials. The "code of silence" is maintained and no union member reports anything negative about a fellow union member.

No consideration is given to the trauma and damage inflicted by the predator on his victim, or the fact that this behavior is unlawful, or the fact that the union official has a legal responsibility to personally report suspected child sexual abuse to the police. Likewise, no consideration is given to future child victims of the predator. Once again, I would label this conduct as unconscionable, unlawful, and warranting a prison term.

<u>Enabling Teachers/Educators</u> who know about or suspect ongoing sexual abuse/harassment but choose to do nothing, have <u>no or low expectations</u> that their actions or lack thereof will result in:

(1) someone filing a complaint with law enforcement against them personally,
(2) someone filing a complaint with the school,
(3) criminal charges and jail time,
(4) civil lawsuits by parents of abused children for monetary damages,
(5) disciplinary action by the school system, or
(6) loss of teaching license.

By remaining silent, enabling teachers/educators avoid negative publicity and protect the school system's "reputation". They also maintain the "code of silence" by not reporting misconduct of a fellow union member. Finally, they maintain positive relations with other teachers and the union, while avoiding the ostracism and retaliation often received by "whistle-blowers."

However, no consideration is given to the welfare or suffering of past, present, and future students at the hands of the sexual predator. Nor is any consideration given to the legal responsibility to personally report suspected child sexual abuse to law enforcement authorities. By remaining silent, enabling teachers/educators are in fact aiding and abetting the criminal sexual abuse of children. Such conduct on the part of any teacher/educator is reprehensible and unlawful, and should result in a prison term. Those for whom the safety and welfare of children is not their foremost priority should not be allowed to work in K-12 institutions or any position that involves child interaction.

Summary

As you can see, the complete lack of expected negative consequences or punishments for child sexual predators, colluding superintendents, colluding union officials, or enabling teachers/educators creates a climate in which sexual abuse/harassment of students will flourish unabated. Unless aggressive steps are taken to hold individuals personally accountable for their conduct and impose strong punishments for unlawful behavior, the pandemic of sexual abuse/harassment in K-12 will continue to victimize millions of innocent students.

The shameless conduct of colluding superintendents, colluding union officials, and enabling teachers/educators makes me wonder if there is any crime committed against innocent children so heinous that they would actually report it to law enforcement. Obviously, the psychologically traumatizing, devastating, and life-long scarring that sexual abuse causes to an innocent child is not enough to cause them to act! If a predator teacher who was sexually abusing young students also tortured and killed them, would they "pass the trash" to another school system, fail to report it to law enforcement, and maintain the code of silence? How much damage has to be done to children before appropriate, legally required action is taken? At what point do these peoples' consciences begin to function? Their collective conduct to date has been disgusting, infuriating, and unlawful. Concerted, aggressive action will be needed to correct this disgraceful problem.

CONCLUSIONS

When I finished writing this chapter, I have to admit feeling somewhat overwhelmed by the number and potency of the inter-related causes of K-12 student sexual abuse/harassment. Taken together, these forces can seem almost insurmountable.

However powerful they are, the need to protect children from sexual abuse/harassment demands a concerted, aggressive response from all of us. There are ways to fight back and insure a safe learning environment for our children. I'll talk specifically about how we can do this in Chapter 10.

CHAPTER 3

KNOWING THE ENEMY—PROFILING ROGUE SEXUAL PREDATORS AND THEIR TECHNIQUES

Below is a self description of the process used by a male teacher and confessed homosexual pedophile (21 victims and over 200 incidents) to "groom" his victims (young boys, 11-14 years old) for abuse, quoted in Teachers That [Who] Sexually Abuse Students (1999, p. 50-52):

"'For a boy to fit my idea of mature, he would exhibit certain physiological features, such as boys go through when in puberty. They would be in that state of growing up but not yet achieving a lot of facial, chest, or pubic hair. A potential victim was normally in that changing voice stage .For a boy to fit my idea of mature, he would have to meet additional physiological conditions such as, he would have to be cute in my estimation, he would have to have a normal build, not too fat nor too skinny, and he would have to be shorter than me. He would also have to have certain personality traits, such as friendly, yet not boisterous; conversational, yet not over talkative; naïve, yet not totally ignorant; bright, yet not necessarily genius; and finally, he would have to indicate a trusting admiration for me.

After I singled out a particular boy, I would begin the process of grooming. This process involved almost the same steps in every case.

I would do a lot of things to gain the boy's confidence. I would explain things extremely carefully or take extra time with him or while explaining things, I would *touch the boy in certain ways to indicate my liking for him, such as a pat or squeeze of his hand. These touching experiences would evolve with the relationship with the boy. In time, I would include hugging and even putting my face against his while leaning over his shoulder to observe his work. There were times when I would wink at him or give him special looks, all of these behaviors I would do as discreetly as possible, as not to arouse any suspicion on the part of the other students. But, looking back, I am sure the others noticed much of my behavior, at least to some degree. Eventually, I would also place special treats on his desk before school began. This would occur after I had developed a relationship with the boy, so he would know where the treats came from. I would also write special coded notes to the boy. After many weeks or months of this type of grooming, I would move into phase two. At this point, I would begin to develop some type of a relationship with the boy's parents. I would groom them in many ways too. If we went to the same church, this was very easy. I would show an interest in helping them in any way that would permit me to become close to them. Soon, they would invite me to their home for dinner, or to go with their family on various outings too: such as hiking, or skiing, or to a movie, or whatever. While involved in their experiences, I would do all within my ability to be a child on his level. I would become very physical with him, in that I would horse around with him, or just plain hold his hand, or even kiss the top of his head to show additional affection, yet nothing distinctly sexual. If for some reason, by accident or by design, we sat beside each other, I would place my foot and/or my leg against his, and I would often place my hand on his leg and squeeze it. I would do all I could to make him think of me as an equal to himself in terms of interests, except that I had a driver's license and a checkbook. . . . At this point I would introduce the subject of sex. I would tell off-colored jokes, or if I already knew the boy's interest in dirty jokes, I might tell even more explicit stories. . . . I would buy Playboy magazines . . . and let him examine them carefully. I would do everything I could to make sex sound like the most fun thing in the world, and that adults always did all they could to keep kids from finding out about this fun. After I was convinced that the boy was groomed sufficiently for some hands-on experience in sex, I would arrange for him to spend some time alone with me. . . . Now I would use one of these outings to talk the boy into allowing me to begin the sexual touching process. Again, I would couch all behavior in the context of what it would be like to have a girl do this. . . .'"*

How disgusting is this? The predator had been a teacher in several school districts, but never faced criminal charges for his illegal behavior. Rather, he was asked to resign and given a positive recommendation for future employment, with no indication in his personnel file of pedophilia or sexual misconduct with students.

Grooming is a technique used in some form by virtually all adults who prey on children. It can be defined as "deliberate actions undertaken to befriend someone (typically a young person or child) with the intent of preparing them for sexual exploitation."

Steps in the grooming process usually include:

1. special attention toward the target victim,
2. special recognition and rewards (verbal praise or small gifts) for the target victim,
3. special privileges and opportunities (for example, invitations for lunch or drinks) for the target victim,
4. slowly increasing the amount of touching and sexual comments to assess the target victim's response and likelihood of resisting or filing a complaint,
5. progressive sexual behavior to desensitize the target victim to what is happening , and further test their resistance and complaint-filing propensity,
6. acts of sexual exploitation/gratification which can recur for months, and in extreme cases, years, and
7. emphasis on the victim's mutual responsibility for the sexual activity and continued need for secrecy.

As I will emphasize in Chapter 6 on avoiding and preventing sexual victimization, if you see or hear that your child is being treated in a special way (being groomed), you need to report it and take aggressive action to stop it immediately. The same applies if you see this happening to another child. It is also critically important to discuss the grooming process with your children and insist that they inform you when it happens to them or another student!

WHO PREYS ON OUR CHILDREN AT SCHOOL

The best data we have about those who sexually abuse/harass K-12 students comes from a national study performed by the American Association of University Women in 2001, entitled "Hostile Hallways". It found that over 80% of the harassment experienced by students at school was initiated by other students. The 2004 Department of Education report, "Educator Sexual Misconduct: A Synthesis of Existing Literature", reanalyzed the AAUW (2001) data and found that 9.6% of the harassment experienced by students was initiated by adult educators. This finding is supported by the AAUW study which noted that 38% of responding students reported that teachers and other school employees sexually harassed students. The Department of Education report goes on to say that, given the position of trust, respect, and authority held by educators, sexual abuse/harassment initiated by them is especially traumatic and damaging to student victims.

Thus, although most sexual abuse/harassment at school is caused by students, I will begin this section with an examination of adult educators (teachers, coaches, administrators, bus drivers, janitors) as sexual abusers/harassers, given their comparatively more devastating impact on victims. After addressing adult abusers/harassers, I will briefly discuss students who harass.

EDUCATORS WHO PREY ON K-12 STUDENTS

Definitions

Pedophilia—*an adult psychosexual disorder evidenced by a strong preference for prepubescent (before puberty) children as sexual partners.*

Hebephilia—*an adult psychosexual disorder evidenced by a strong preference for pubescent (going through puberty) or young post-pubescent adolescents as sexual partners.*

<u>Child Sexual Abuse</u>—*illegal sexual contact or conduct involving an adult and a child (underage person, with the age of consent varying from state to state—often 18 years old).*

Let me be perfectly clear about educators who sexually abuse/harass K-12 students. They are corrupt individuals who knowingly, willingly, enthusiastically, and repeatedly engage in unlawful sexual conduct with children, typically resulting in profound damage to their young victims. They prey on the innocent, the powerless, and the vulnerable for their sexual satisfaction. They are a blight on the entire education profession. As I will discuss in Chapter 10 on correcting this problem, child sexual abusers/harassers should be prevented from entering the profession, aggressively prosecuted if they violate the law, and banned from the profession for violations of the law.

Statistics from a variety of sources indicate that sexual abusers/harassers of K-12 students are overwhelmingly male, nearly 90%. The Department of Education report entitled, "Educator Sexual Misconduct: A Synthesis of The Literature" (2004, p.25), described this phenomenon as a "monopoly by male abusers". In the largest study of its kind, Dr. Gene Abel analyzed responses to over 600 questions from 4,000 admitted child sexual abusers. The results are reported in the book, <u>Stop Child Molestation</u> (2001), by Dr. Abel and Nora Harlow. Within the sample of abusers, 99% were male and only 1% female.

There are certainly cases involving female teachers as sexual abusers/harassers, and they often receive significant media attention. Perhaps the most notorious case is that of Mary Kay Letourneau, in the late 1990's. She served seven years in prison for the statutory rape of a 13-year-old boy and had his child. Upon release, she violated terms of her sentence and was discovered in a car with the same boy. Letourneau was sent back to jail, where she gave birth to a second child by the young boy. Upon her final release from prison, she and the boy were married, and wrote a book, followed by a movie about their experience. Nevertheless, K-12 predators are predominately male.

Based upon a national survey he conducted and his treatment of child sex offenders, clinical psychologist Dr. Stephen Rubin (coauthor of <u>Teachers That [Who] Sexually Abuse Students,</u> 1999) noted the following characteristics or risk factors associated with these predators:

(1) an employment record showing frequent job changes, especially in different states,
(2) the absence of normal peer relationships with other adults,

(3) a preference for social contact with children,
(4) a gregarious and outgoing personality, often found among "coaches, counselors, music teachers, drama teachers, and art teachers." (p. 123),
(5) a primary interest in the teaching profession due to the easy access to children and position of power and authority, and
(6) devious and scheming in pursuing their targets.

From <u>Educators That [Who] Sexually Abuse Students</u> (p.5):

"In at least one case, a homosexual pedophile took classes, at his employing school district's expense, on how to identify the homosexual pedophile. He then used this new knowledge in order to avoid detection."

Particularly disturbing is the following quote from the Department of Education report entitled, "Educator Sexual Misconduct: A Synthesis of Existing Literature" (2004, p. 31 and 32):

"In elementary schools, the abuser is often one of the people that students most like and that parents most trust. The abusers of children younger than seventh grade have different patterns than those who abuse older children (Shakeshaft, 2003). The educators who target elementary school children are often professionally accomplished and even celebrated. Particularly compared to their non-abusing counterparts, they hold a disproportionate number of awards. It is common to find that educators who have been sexually abusing children are also the same educators who display on their walls a community "Excellence in Teaching" award or a "Teacher of the Year" certificate. This popularity confounds district officials and community members and prompts them to ignore allegations on the belief that 'outstanding teachers' cannot be abusers.

Many educators who abuse work at being recognized as good professionals in order to be able to sexually abuse children. For them, being a good educator is the path to children, especially those who abuse elementary and younger middle school students." (Shakeshaft and Cohan, 1994)

This report also noted that "teachers whose job description includes time with individual students, such as music teachers or coaches, are more likely to sexually abuse than other teachers" (p.22). Finally, the report concluded that most abusers are serial or "chronic predators".

My own research, experience, and interaction with sexual predators at the college level suggest that they share many of the same flaws with teachers who prey on K-12 students. The list includes:

Immoral and Dishonest   Sexual abusers/harassers typically have weak or nonexistent moral standards that allow them to rationalize their illegal conduct and feel no remorse or guilt. They have the capacity to lie in a very convincing and compelling manner. This allows them to easily deflect victim complaints, if they occur, and redirect attention to the "false" allegation by the student.

High Comfort Level with the Dominator Role The warped personalities of sexual abusers/ harassers motivate them to seek victims whom they can dominate and control. In their roles as teachers, with clear authority over students, these predators relish the misuse of this power to victimize young people and satisfy their sexual appetites.

Clear Grasp of Gate Keeper Function With older students, typically in high school, predators clearly recognize their critical role in facilitating student progress and advancement. Grades, honors and awards, recommendations for college and/or employment, selection for scholarships, and recommendations for special academic programs are all important outcomes that teachers control. The high degree of control that teachers have over students' futures can be emphasized to potential victims to force their compliance.

Knowledge of School Functioning K-12 predators usually have a clear grasp of how schools function and ways to take advantage of this to conceal and protect their illicit activities. For example, they know that: (1) school administrators are unlikely to believe a student complaint if convincingly denied by the predator, (2) teachers' unions will blindly support any predator, no matter how heinous their crimes, (3) school administrators are primarily interested in protecting their own careers and the reputation of the school district, and (4) with pressure from teachers' unions, most administrators will not make legally required reports to law enforcement officials, will not discipline the offender, but will provide a positive letter of reference to the predator if he agrees to resign. Predators use the above knowledge to continue to prey on unsuspecting victims with impunity, fully believing that, if caught, they will simply move on to another school district.

Serial Abusers/Harassers The overwhelming majority of K-12 sexual abusers/harassers are serial offenders. They repeatedly victimize multiple young people throughout their careers, until they are stopped and either incarcerated (for criminal offenses) or banned from the profession (for civil offenses).

The common response from predators to conclusive evidence of unlawful behavior is that it was the first and only time that such a mistake was made. These lies are offered to suggest that their "first-time" offense should result in little or no disciplinary action. The truth of the matter is, this was only the first time they were caught, and their unlawful behavior with students has been occurring throughout their careers.

<u>Social Radar</u> One very disgusting characteristic of many predators is their uncanny ability to identify target victims who appear to be passive, timid, vulnerable, emotionally needy, submissive to authority, likely to submit to sexual advances, and unlikely to make a complaint. Predators use a variety of information to make these judgments including family situation, past academic performance and conduct grades, and current verbal and nonverbal behaviors. Based upon their assessment of this information, they target the most defenseless children to pursue. How evil is this?

Common Techniques

Dziech and Weiner wrote a groundbreaking book in 1984 called <u>The Lecherous Professor</u> (a second edition appeared in 1990). The authors discussed the most common techniques used by faculty predators with college students. These techniques are also used by K-12 predators. A full understanding of the approaches used to victimize students can hopefully help you and your child to quickly identify and resist them, and report the perpetrator's conduct.

<u>Gate Keeper/Power Broker</u> As mentioned earlier in this chapter, teachers do have significant influence over the academic and employment futures of their students. This influence is most evident and pronounced in high school, when young people are preparing to go to college or find employment. Many predators are quite blatant and direct in communicating to students that their sexual cooperation and silence are prerequisites before receiving: (1) a good grade in the class needed to maintain a high GPA, (2) a positive recommendation for college, employment, an internship, or a scholarship, (3) a designation as a "first chair" in the school orchestra, (4) an artistic award, or (5) an opportunity to participate in a prestigious academic program. Students are also often warned that filing

a complaint would result in dire consequences, and that no one would believe them or their story. Clearly, this predator strategy is a flagrant abuse of power to satisfy sexual needs.

Intellectual Seducer This tactic is also used most frequently with older students, typically in high school. It is more subtle than the Gate Keeper approach described above, but equally devastating. It begins by showering intellectual flattery on an unsuspecting low self-esteem student, both publicly in class and in private. The intent is to first intellectually seduce the young woman and then take advantage of her sexually. The intense attention and recognition shown by a prominent teacher can be overwhelming, ego enhancing, and very difficult to resist.

Counselor/Advisor Another subtle yet powerful abuse/harassment approach involves the bastardization of the teacher's legitimate role as a counselor or advisor. Sexual predators exploit unsuspecting, often emotionally troubled, and immature students who seek advice by taking advantage of their vulnerability. Frequently, this begins by the predator displaying apparently genuine feelings of concern and empathy for a student, thus winning her confidence and trust. Once achieved, sexual advances quickly follow.

Confidant/Friend Predators who use this approach attempt to befriend unsuspecting, often socially isolated, and shy students by initially treating them as equals and sharing intimate personal information. This strategy is often implemented at offsite, non-school locations like restaurants, parties, or even the harasser's apartment/home. Once the predator has won the confidence and friendship of his victim, he moves quickly to exploit this trust with his sexual advances.

Opportunist Abusers/harassers using this technique engage in apparently harmless, yet sexually provocative and inappropriate touching of students, commenting about their appearance or personal lives, and sharing sexually explicit jokes and stories. Often disguised as humor, these tactics are intended to solicit expressions of interest on the part of students, typically in middle school or high school. The predator then quickly takes advantage of these opportunities by pursuing those who show interest.

Hybrid Techniques While the five approaches described above are relatively unique and independent, some sexual predators utilize a combined or hybrid strategy to exploit their prey. For example, an abuser/harasser might begin with the Intellectual Seducer approach and then at the right time, follow with the Gate Keeper/Power Broker technique, explicitly offering a passing grade or recommendation in exchange for sex.

The Special Case of Coaches Who Abuse/Harass

The problem of male athletic coaches who sexually abuse/harass female students is widespread and persistent throughout the country, especially at the middle school and high school levels. Clinical psychologist Stephen Rubin (co-author of <u>Teachers That [Who] Sexually Abuse Students</u>) asserted that his research shows that coaches are the most common sexual abusers of students after grade school. According to an investigation by the Seattle Times (December 16, 2003), data collected by the Washington Office of Superintendent of Public Instruction revealed that teachers who coach are three times more likely to be accused of and investigated for sexual abuse of students than non-coaching teachers.

The newspaper (December 14, 2003) also provided the following details of a notorious case involving a coach and a young female player:

"The bond between athlete and coach can be powerful, and the one between a 15-year-old Port Townsend girl and a 34-year-old basketball coach was especially strong. The girl, raised in a trouble home, saw Randy Sheriff not only as a mentor on dribbling and jump-shooting, but as a surrogate parent, confidant and 'the greatest dad in the world.' Sheriff showered her first with attention, then with flowers and chocolates, then with kisses.

Before long, the coach – a married man with two children of his own – was sending the teenager love notes. By the time she was 16, she said, she and the coach were having sex in his car, at his house and in motels. Occasionally, she said, he brought along alcohol and marijuana they both used. People around them suspected as much but looked the other way as Sheriff isolated the girl from her friends and family. The relationship took its toll on her. Because Sheriff insisted on secrecy, the teenager distanced herself from family and friends, feeling alone and ashamed.

'If we were driving where people might see us, he would put my head down on the seat of the car until we got out of town,' she later said in a statement. 'That was extremely humiliating for me.' The girl slipped into depression and had suicidal thoughts."

Ironically, since the passage of Title IX in 1972, which required equal treatment of males and females in schools receiving any federal funding, sports opportunities for girls in high school and college have expanded dramatically. Unfortunately, many of the coaches of girls' sports teams in middle school and high school are men.

Male coaches with a winning record, who have helped players land lucrative college scholarships are in great demand. Disgustingly, administrators and even parents often ignore complaints against successful coaches.

Given the widespread abuse of female players by male coaches, clearly aggressive corrective strategies are needed. As I will discuss later in the book, I recommend banning men from holding jobs coaching female students. This would deny them the opportunity to sexually abuse their players. At the very least, every male coach should have an adult female co-coach, who is present during all interaction with female players.

Other Adult Sexual Abusers/Harassers

In addition to teachers, any adult in a school setting with access to children has the potential to be a sexual abuser/harasser. This includes principals, counselors, librarians, janitors, bus drivers, nurses, security guards, and volunteers. Below are specific cases that illustrate how serious this problem is.

According to the Christian Science Monitor, February 2, 2012: "In the late 1990's, Jeremy Bell {student} was sexually assaulted by his school principal and at one point was given a chemical to render him defenseless, which turned out to be lethal. Parents and teachers had reported the principal to the school board, and he had moved across state lines multiple times for jobs."

According to the Minneapolis News, February 22, 2012, former teacher's aide, Michelle Rose Chlan, at Shakopee Junior High School was sentenced to 90 days in jail for felony third-degree criminal sexual conduct for having oral sex with a male student in a Kmart parking lot. Chlan often gave the young boy rides home from school.

In a case in North Carolina, a female mentally disabled student was reportedly sexually abused by a janitor, who defended his conduct by claiming that she welcomed the sex, that he had no formal authority over her, and thus had done nothing wrong.

In the book, <u>Teachers That {Who} Sexually Abuse Students</u> (1999), the authors discuss a case involving a school bus driver for elementary-age children who repeatedly sexually abused young girls as they sat in his lap or beside him. The driver also frequently stopped the bus along the road side, apparently to concentrate more on his helpless victims.

Any adult with access to students has the opportunity to abuse. This includes volunteers, as illustrated in the following case from the Government Accountability Office (2010, p.6) report on sexual misconduct in schools:

"A Florida public school allowed an individual who was convicted of having sex with an underage male to work as a volunteer coach without a criminal history check, even though school policy provided that volunteers would be subject to such checks. He was eventually arrested for having sexual contact with a student on one of the school's sports teams."

Students as Sexual Harassers/Abusers

The American Association of University Women report in 2001, "Hostile Hallways: Bullying, Teasing, and Sexual Harassment in School", concluded that the majority of all sexual harassment occurs between students. However, only a small percentage of the harassment could be categorized as criminal sexual abuse. Verbal comments, teasing, cyber-messages, and incidental physical contact are much more common.

Having said this, it is critically important that rogue students who engage in sexual misconduct be quickly identified and referred to treatment facilities and alternative juvenile school programs. Ideally, schools with clear student conduct and dress code guidelines, zero-tolerance policies, and effective monitoring programs can identify problematic behaviors before they become serious and initiate effective corrective/disciplinary action.

In a recent case in California, two elementary school sisters were attacked by a group of male classmates, who restrained them in chokeholds, pinched and tripped them, and grabbed their chests, genitalia and buttocks. Complaints by the parents resulted in the boys receiving only verbal warnings not to do these things again. Later that school year, six boys, including some involved in the earlier assault, threw the two girls to the ground, forcibly kissed and fondled them, and tried to remove their clothes.

Clearly, the young boys involved in these attacks needed to be removed from the public schools and referred for treatment and alternative schooling.

Schools often go to great lengths to protect their star athletes from allegations of sexual abuse/ harassment. While this problem is especially pronounced in college (as evidenced by recent cases at the University of Montana and University of Georgia), it is also prevalent at the high school level. Consider the following case reported by the Courthouse News Service, June 5, 2012:

"Williamsport, PA — A girl claims in Federal Court that her school district and high school principal protected two star athletes who sexually assaulted her, defended them at every turn even after they had been found guilty, and violated a court order protecting her.

She claims that 'the school district has adopted and enforced a disciplinary system designed to protect and maintain athletic eligibility for its male athletes regardless of their criminal behavior and/or propensity for violence against female students.'"

Sexual harassment/abuse initiated by students most often arises in schools that unwittingly create a "climate of abuse". Elements include: (1) teachers who sexually harass/abuse students without disciplinary consequences (38% of students in the 2001 AAUW national survey reported seeing teachers sexually harass students), (2) a failure on the part of administrators and teachers to monitor and correct inappropriate student behaviors (the 2001 AAUW report, p. 32, stated, "In several studies, students noted that even when sexual harassment happens right in front of teachers, few teachers do anything about it"), (3) a lack of significant disciplinary consequences for students engaged in sexually harassing conduct, and (4) a failure to enforce dress codes.

The obvious solution is a strictly enforced zero-tolerance policy with significant disciplinary consequences for violators, up to and including expulsion. Without appropriate policies/rules in place, ongoing monitoring, and effective enforcement, student-on-student sexual abuse/harassment incidence rates will be high.

CONCLUSIONS

You and your daughters and sons need to clearly understand the kinds of people who are most likely to sexually abuse students and the tactics that they use. If your daughter or son feels that they have been targeted for sexual abuse/harassment or grooming, they need to bring this to your attention immediately. You then need to initiate aggressive corrective action with school officials and if criminal conduct has occurred, report it to law enforcement authorities.

We need to teach our children to be aware of their surroundings and how other people are treating them. When your child is inappropriately treated, you need to be informed. It is also a good idea for you to conduct your own independent observations of how your child acts and is treated in school, by the teacher and other students.

CHAPTER 4

EDUCATORS WHO ENABLE, AID, AND ABET CRIMINAL CHILD SEXUAL ABUSERS AND ABANDON VICTIMS

Edmund Burke: "All that is necessary for the triumph of evil is that good men {and women} do nothing."

While the overwhelming majority of school administrators, union officials, and teachers/educators would never consider sexually abusing/harassing a student, the same overwhelming majority would never consider filing and have never filed a legally required police complaint against a teacher who was suspected of sexually abusing/harassing students. They choose instead to maintain a strict code of silence and let administrators secretly negotiate "passing the trash" deals to send the predator to another school district.

Herein lies a substantial cause of the pandemic of sexual abuse/harassment of K-12 students. Sexual abuse/harassment occurs because the overwhelming majority of school administrators, union officials, and teachers/educators choose to ignore the problem and remain silent.

In a 2008 case reported by www.abajournal.com/news, the Seattle Public Schools agreed to pay $3.5 million to two students molested by a former 5th-grade teacher during his 20-year education career, involving multiple victims. According to the attorney representing the two students: "<u>It was kind of the open secret within</u>

<u>Broadview-Thompson Elementary School. The teachers knew about it, but parents didn't know about it. The police didn't know about it."</u>

From my perspective, all of these teachers who failed to fulfill their legal responsibility to report suspected child abuse to the police are just as guilty as the predator and should also face criminal changes. Sexually abusing/harassing students is illegal. Anyone who knows about and fails to report it is an accessory to the crime and is aiding and abetting the criminal.

IMPORTANT QUESTIONS FOR EVERY EDUCATOR

Given the pandemic incidence of sexual abuse/harassment of K-12 students and the staggering number of 4.5 million student victims of educator sexual misconduct estimated by the U.S. Department of Education (2004), two critically important and appropriate questions to pose to every educator are:

1. How many complaints have you personally filed against other school employees (teachers, administrators, counselors, coaches, janitors, etc.) for sexually abusing students?
2. How many times have you referred a suspected child victim of educator sexual abuse for counseling or other assistance?

Every state has laws requiring anyone with reason to believe that child sexual abuse has occurred or is occurring to personally report it to state child welfare or law enforcement authorities, and many states have anonymous tip lines for abuse reporting. Thus, every educator has a <u>personal</u> <u>legal</u> responsibility to report suspected child sexual abuse, in addition to a moral and professional responsibility. Doesn't every educator have a moral and professional responsibility to protect children from being injured and get them help if they are harmed?

Tragically, in spite of this unambiguous legal responsibility to report suspected child sexual abuse and widespread access to anonymous tip lines, the Department of Education report, "Educator Sexual Misconduct: A Synthesis of Existing Literature" (2004), concluded: "<u>Seldom</u> is the abuse reported by a teacher, <u>even if the child had told the teacher</u> [emphasis added]" (p.34), and (p.35) "When alleged misconduct is reported, the majority of complaints are ignored or disbelieved."

How outrageously unconscionable is this? Turning your back on a helpless child complaining about a sexual predator. Regardless of the reason(s) for this conduct, in my opinion, anyone with knowledge or reasonable suspicion of child sexual abuse who fails to report it is just as guilty as the predator and should face criminal charges! They are allowing child sexual abuse to continue and refusing to get help for victims. How do these people sleep at night? How do they live with themselves and justify their failure to report and get help for victims?

As coauthor John Biggs (school system attorney) of <u>Teachers That [Who] Sexually Abuse Students</u> (1999) notes, administrators and fellow teachers typically deny they had any knowledge of ongoing sexual abuse. He states that they do not see or hear because they do not want to see or hear. The K-12 school system is further described as (p.17), "Not just an ostrich with its head in the sand, it is an ostrich which dons blinders and earplugs before putting its head in the sand." Given the widespread prevalence of student sexual abuse in K-12, most educators who have been in the profession for several years are likely to have encountered instances of educator sexual misconduct, failed to report it, and failed to get help for victims. People worry about what their coworkers might say if they report suspected child sexual abuse, or what the teachers' union might say, or what the administration might say, or how bad the publicity will be for the school. Never once does the welfare of children enter into this thought process! How shameful! These cowardly educators sacrifice the present and long-term welfare of children for the sake of protecting themselves and their colleagues who prey on young victims.

The safety and welfare of children must be the number one priority of everyone in education. Anyone who jeopardizes the safety and welfare of children must be dealt with swiftly and decisively!

Reporting suspected child sexual abuse is a necessary first step in this process. It does not matter who threatens the safety and welfare of children, they must be reported. Furthermore, suspected victims of sexual abuse must get the help that they need to cope and recover.

Unfortunately, repercussions will typically follow for those who report colleagues. Whistleblowers are often scorned, ridiculed, and shunned by their coworkers and administrators. In my opinion, this is a small price to pay for aggressively protecting student safety and welfare.

I started this section with two important questions that should be posed to every educator:

1. How many complaints have you personally filed against other school employees (teachers, administrators, counselors, coaches, janitors, etc.) for sexually abusing students?
2. How many times have you referred a suspected child victim of educator sexual abuse for counseling or other assistance?

For most teachers, if they have been in the education field for several years, it is likely that they have been exposed to instances of suspected child sexual abuse by their colleagues. Thus, <u>if</u> this is true, and they have not reported it to law enforcement and child protective authorities, they are accessories to the crime and a huge part of the K-12 problem. I expect teachers to put student safety first, and I'm sure I speak for all parents on this issue.

I have taught college classes for 34 years. During this time, when students tell me they are being sexually abused or harassed by another faculty member, I file a formal written complaint with my university or directly with the police, if I believe a crime may have been committed and make referrals concerning mental health providers. Over my career, I have: (1) filed 6 complaints with my university against professors, (2) filed 1 complaint with the Office for Civil Rights in the U.S. Department of Education, (3) filed 1 police complaint, (4) provided sworn testimony in a federal court case against my school and a sexually abusive professor, and (5) worked with attorneys representing students in two cases against faculty at my school.

I expect the same level of commitment to student safety and welfare from any professional in education! If someone isn't willing to do this, my advice is to find work in another field before tougher laws are enacted to criminalize the failure to report child sexual abuse!

As I said earlier, there are always consequences for whistleblowers. I was told many times that I would never be promoted to full professor—the angry faculty "good old boys' club" and administration would see to that. My family was threatened, forcing us to move to another state, so I have a

200-mile round-trip commute to work. I will never win a popularity contest among our faculty and I always watch my back. I do know who my real friends and supporters are, and I sleep soundly at night. I also know that I have made a difference on my campus in protecting student safety and civil rights.

Thus, without hesitation, I can ask any K-12 educator who has been in the field for several years, how many complaints have you filed on behalf of students concerning suspected child sexual abuse and how many suspected student victims have you referred for treatment. For many educators, silence or indignation tells me loudly and clearly that these cowards have been aiding and abetting the criminal sexual abuse of children by their predator colleagues masquerading as teachers. They have also abandoned helpless children by allowing the abuse to continue and failing to get treatment for current and past victims.

This is unacceptable to me and any parent. Aggressive corrective action is needed and needed now!

CONCLUSIONS

I urge you to hold all educators accountable for the horrible problem of teacher sexual abuse of K-12 students. Certainly the predators themselves are guilty, but so too are the other educators who enable this criminal conduct, sometimes for many years without ever reporting it!

Child safety and welfare must be the number one priority of every educator. No one or nothing should be allowed to harm children at school! All threats to child safety and welfare must be dealt with aggressively and decisively!

CHAPTER 5

ADVOCATING FOR YOUR CHILD — KNOW YOUR LEGAL RIGHTS

In a recent case reported in Kentucky, a 13-year-old 8th-grade girl was allegedly sexually assaulted by an 18-year-old male student who was a star athlete at the school. After filing a complaint with school authorities, it is alleged that no investigation took place nor was appropriate disciplinary action taken. It is also alleged that school officials were aware of two previous sexual assaults by the 18- year-old involving other female students. Finally, it is alleged that, after filing the complaint, the young girl faced retaliation and harassment from other students and school employees. Courthouse New Service, August 26, 2011 (www.courthousenews.com)

How would you react if you were the parent of this young girl? After your anger and rage subsided, you would probably consider taking legal action. This case and others like it are often very complicated, and offer multiple legal options.

There is no substitute for sound legal advice from a competent attorney, with prior experience dealing with such cases. Finding such an attorney can be challenging. A recommended first step is to contact your local city, county, or state bar (a professional association of lawyers) and request the names of attorneys who practice/specialize in this area. For example, the National Crime Victim Bar Association provides a referral service to local lawyers specializing in victim-related litigation, including child sexual abuse. Specific referrals can be obtained by calling (202) 467-8716. The organization's web address is www.victimbar.org.

You can then contact the recommended individuals to determine if they are qualified to represent you and your daughter/son. I can't emphasize enough how important it is to hire an attorney with extensive prior experience with these types of cases. The last thing you and your family need is a lawyer who is unfamiliar with this area of the law and learning about it as your case progresses.

For example, most people would never consider asking a general surgeon to perform her/his first brain surgery on your child. You'd want an experienced brain surgeon in the first place. Use this same approach in finding an experienced attorney.

INTRODUCTION

In this chapter I will provide you with general information about the laws that pertain to sexual harassment and sexual abuse in school settings. First, I will discuss federal civil rights legislation and then consider state laws pertinent to both potential civil and criminal charges. My goal is to help you become an informed advocate for your child. I will present the various specific complaint filing options in the next chapter, and identify pros and cons of each one.

FEDERAL CIVIL RIGHTS

Title IX

<u>Major Provisions</u> The federal statute that provides the specific legal framework for addressing sexual harassment in school settings is Title IX of the Education Amendments of 1972. Major features of Title IX include:

- prohibits discrimination in education on the basis of an individual's sex,
- no specific reference to sexual harassment,
- applies to any educational program or activity receiving federal funding,
- directs each individual federal department or agency involved in providing financial assistance to any educational program/activity to "effectuate" compliance with Title IX, and
- no specific reference to a private right to sue.

Office for Civil Rights (OCR)

The official enforcement agency for Title IX is the Office for Civil Rights (OCR). It was established by administrative action, within the newly formed Department of Education in 1980, upon dissolution of the federal Department of Health, Education, and Welfare. Beginning in 1992, the OCR has published a series of guidelines on compliance with Title IX, including:

1. Nondiscrimination on the Basis of Sex in Education Programs and Activities Receiving or Benefiting from Federal Financial Assistance, 1992,
2. Sexual Harassment Guidance: Harassment of Students by School Employees, Other Students or Third Parties, 1997, revised, 2001,
3. Dear Colleague Letter, Sexual Harassment Issues, 2006,
4. Sexual Harassment: It's Not Academic (Revised), 2008,
5. OCR Case Processing Manual (CPM) (Revised), 2010,
6. Dear Colleague Letter, Guidance on Civil Rights Responsibility for Bullying and Harassment, 2010, and
7. Dear Colleague Letter, Sexual Violence Guidance, 2011.

The OCR defines sexual harassment as unwelcome conduct of a sexual nature that denies or limits a student's ability to participate in or benefit from a school's education program. The 2011 Dear Colleague Letter emphasized that sexual violence is also a form of unlawful harassment.

<u>Three Procedural Requirements</u> Based upon the OCR guidelines, there are three procedural requirements that schools receiving federal funding must meet in order to comply with Title IX. Quoting directly from the OCR's Dear Colleague Letter, Sexual Violence Guidance (2011, p. 6-8), the three requirements include:

"1. Disseminate a notice of nondiscrimination.

The Title IX regulations require that each recipient publish a notice of nondiscrimination stating that the recipient does not discriminate on the basis of sex in its education programs and activities, and that Title IX requires it not to discriminate in such a manner. The notice must state that inquiries concerning the application of Title IX may be referred to the recipient's Title IX coordinator or to OCR. It should include the name or title, office address, telephone number, and e-mail address for the recipient's designated Title IX coordinator.

The notice must be widely distributed to all students, parents of elementary and secondary students, employees, applicants for admission and employment, and other relevant persons. OCR recommends that the notice be prominently posted on school Web sites and at various locations throughout the school or campus and published in electronic and printed publications of general distribution that provide information to students and employees about the school's services and policies. The notice should be available and easily accessible on an ongoing basis.

Title IX does not require a recipient to adopt a policy specifically prohibiting sexual harassment or sexual violence. As noted in the 2001 Guidance, however, a recipient's general policy prohibiting sex discrimination will not be considered effective and would violate Title IX if, because of the lack of a specific policy, students are unaware of what kind of conduct constitutes sexual harassment, including sexual violence, or that such conduct is prohibited sex discrimination.

2. Designate at least one employee to coordinate its efforts to comply with and carry out its responsibilities under Title IX.

The Title IX regulations require a recipient to notify all students and employees of the name or title and contact information of the person designated to coordinate the recipient's compliance with

Title IX. The coordinator's responsibilities include overseeing all Title IX complaints and identifying and addressing any patterns or systemic problems that arise during the review of such complaints. The Title IX coordinator or designee should be available to meet with students as needed.

3. Adopt and publish grievance procedures providing for prompt and equitable resolution of student and employee sex discrimination complaints.

   The Title IX regulations require all recipients to adopt and publish grievance procedures providing for the prompt and equitable resolution of sex discrimination complaints. The grievance procedures must apply to sex discrimination complaints filed by students against school employees, other students, or third parties.

   Title IX does not require a recipient to provide separate grievance procedures for sexual harassment and sexual violence complaints. Therefore, a recipient may use student disciplinary procedures or other separate procedures to resolve such complaints. Any procedures used to adjudicate complaints of sexual harassment or sexual violence, including disciplinary procedures, however must meet the Title IX requirement of affording a complainant a prompt and equitable resolution. These requirements are discussed in greater detail below. If the recipient relies on disciplinary procedures for Title IX compliance, the Title IX coordinator should review the recipient's disciplinary procedures to ensure that the procedures comply with the prompt and equitable requirements of Title IX."

In addition to the above three requirements, OCR publications offer several recommendations to schools concerning compliance with Title IX. These include specific suggestions concerning prevention, investigation, and correction of sexual harassment.

Enforcement Activities   The OCR is authorized to engage in several specific enforcement activities related to Title IX. Among the most important are:

- receive and process student complaints,
- investigate complaints,
- independently initiate compliance reviews without a complaint,

- negotiate voluntary complaint resolutions and issue commitments to resolve,
- monitor compliance with resolution agreements,
- mediate complaints,
- issue "letters of finding" if an educational institution is found to be in noncompliance or declines to reach a voluntary agreement,
- recommend suspension or termination of federal funding for offending educational institutions,
- issue school compliance guidelines,
- refer cases to the Department of Justice for legal action, and
- provide technical assistance to schools/colleges to facilitate compliance.

<u>Operation and Effectiveness</u> Unfortunately, the OCR is generally considered to be operationally ineffective in protecting K-12 students from sexual abuse/harassment. A few statistics will document this deeply disappointing performance failure.

First, although the OCR is empowered to request that a school's federal funding be suspended or terminated due to noncompliance with Title IX, it has <u>never</u> been used by the OCR in a sexual harassment case. I confirmed this fact in a phone conversation with an OCR staff attorney on 27 January 2012. Schools know that federal funding has never been suspended or terminated in 32 years (since OCR's inception in 1980) and is certainly unlikely to happen in the future. Thus, the OCR's enforcement authority is essentially nonexistent.

Second, in response to my written Freedom of Information Act request, the OCR reported that in FY 2008 (the most recent year available), 69 sexual harassment complaints were received from the approximately 78.0 million students covered by Title IX (49.8 million in K-12 and 18.2 million in college). Thus, the percentage of students filing sexual harassment complaints in 2008 with the OCR was a microscopic .000088%.

Third and last, my review of the 69 sexual harassment complaints submitted to the OCR indicated that <u>none</u> of the students were in K-12. How pathetic is this? The OCR is a total nonentity for K-12 students in the United States, and this is the official federal government agency charged with protecting students' civil rights in our country!

JUDICIAL INTERPRETATION IN TITLE IX CASES—MAJOR SUPREME COURT DECISIONS

There have been six important Supreme Court decisions involving Title IX lawsuits initiated by students. These decisions have had a significant impact on how helpful and useful Title IX is to students seeking justice with sexual discrimination complaints against schools. The names, dates, and major elements of these six Supreme Court opinions include:

1. Cannon v. University of Chicago (1979)
   - for the first time, the Supreme Court formally recognized that student victims have an implied right of action (are able to sue) under Title IX.

2. Franklin v. Gwinnett County Public Schools (1992)
   - established that a private plaintiff (student) could seek monetary damages from a school (not individual teachers or administrators) for violation of Title IX, and
   - the decision provided no guidelines or standards for determining school liability.

3. Gebser v. Lago Independent School District (1998)
   - established two specific criteria for determining school liability for teacher harassment of students:
     (1) a senior school official, with the authority to address and correct the harassment, must have <u>actual knowledge</u> of the discrimination, and
     (2) the school responded to the harassment complaint in a "deliberately indifferent" manner.

4. Davis v. Monroe County Board of Education (1999)
   - extended the Gebser v. Lago (1998) decision to include student-on-student harassment,
   - defined "deliberate indifference" as a school's response (or lack of a response) that is clearly unreasonable in light of the known circumstances in the case, and

- stipulated that sexual harassment is actionable (a student can file a lawsuit) only if it is "so severe, pervasive, and objectively offensive" that it effectively bars the victim's access to an educational opportunity or benefit at the school.

5. Jackson v. Birmingham Board of Education (2005)
- confirmed that Title IX also protects students from retaliation and differential treatment for filing a complaint.

6. Fitzgerald v. Barnstable School Committee (2009)
- ruled that student complaints of sexual harassment were not restricted to filing as Title IX violations and
- expanded filing options for students to include action under 42 U.S.C. §1983, which allows for legal action against individual school teachers/employees and administrators.

Given the above Supreme Court decisions, here are the four elements that you must prove in order to establish that a violation of Title IX has occurred:

1. the school receives federal funding (virtually all public schools and many private schools receive funding from the federal government),
2. the unwelcome sexual harassment must be so severe, pervasive, and objectively offensive that it deprives the victim of access to educational opportunities or benefits offered by the school,
3. actual knowledge of the harassment on the part of a senior school official with the authority to address the alleged discrimination and institute corrective action, and
4. "deliberate indifference" on the part of the school to the student's complaint – a response that is "clearly unreasonable in light of the known circumstances".

Taken together, the last three requirements make it exceedingly difficult for students to prevail in Title IX cases against schools—not impossible, but very challenging. For some inexplicable reason(s), the federal government makes it more difficult for students to win sexual harassment cases against schools than it is for employees to win against employers.

As noted earlier in Chapter 2, the Vice President for Education and Employment at the National Women's Law Center, Fatima Goss-Graves, made the following comments (p.7) to the U.S. Commission on Civil Rights (May 13, 2011):

"The effect of the Supreme Court's decisions in Gebser and Davis cannot be overstated. Simply put, these decisions have substantially hampered the ability of private litigants to receive full compensation under Title IX for their injuries resulting from past sexual harassment. School that ignore harassment can increasingly act with impunity."

One promising approach to demonstrating that a school has been "deliberately indifferent" to a sexual harassment complaint is to produce evidence that the school had knowledge of past sexual misconduct on the part of the harasser. Since many, if not most, harassers are serial abusers, it can often be easier to document previous instances of sexual misconduct than you might think.

For example, in the Kentucky case cited at the beginning of this chapter, the school allegedly had prior knowledge of two sexual assaults by the harasser and did nothing to prevent future attacks on young girls. If proved at trial, this could be interpreted as deliberate indifference by the school.

To illustrate how prior sexual misconduct and "deliberate indifference" can be related, I will use a case in which I testified against my university and another faculty member, involving the sexual assault of a student in the professor's office. Federal District Judge Lozano described the assault in his opinion: "Rhea forcibly grabbed her. He tried to kiss her on the mouth and put his tongue in her mouth. He pulled up her shirt and bra, grabbed at her breasts, and put his mouth on them. He grabbed her buttocks and started moving his hand around to her genitals."

The judge noted that Rhea had multiple instances of previous sexual misconduct with students. The university had not taken effective disciplinary/corrective action in response to Rhea's sexual misconduct or steps to prevent similar misconduct in the future. The judge asserted that: "The student body was never informed that Rhea had sexually harassed students or that he had been reprimanded for doing so." In conclusion, the judge stated: "On these facts, a reasonable jury could find that the university was deliberately indifferent." This is known as "before-the-fact deliberate indifference". Chontos v. Rhea, 29F. Supp. 2d. 931 (1998), No. 2:97-CV-423-RL

Clearly, any student (college or K-12) who has been sexually abused/harassed can establish "before-the-fact deliberate indifference" by a school, if the perpetrator, whether school employee or student, had a prior record of sexual misconduct that was known to school officials. In these instances, the institution should have taken aggressive steps to prevent such sexual misconduct from reoccurring in the future and protect students from serial offenders.

When schools have knowledge of previous sexual misconduct on the part of an alleged abuser/harasser, a school's failure to protect all students from harm, in my opinion, demonstrates criminal before-the-fact indifference, not merely deliberate indifference. From my perspective, administrators who choose not to protect students from a known risk should face criminal charges.

Retaliation

As noted above, the Supreme Court, in the Jackson v Birmingham (2005) case, confirmed that Title IX offers protection to complainants from retaliation. School attorney and co-author of <u>Educators That [Who] Sexually Abuse Students</u>, John Biggs, made the following important points about retaliation (p. 184):

"A person who complains of sexual harassment is protected against any sort of retaliatory discrimination. A teacher or staff person who somehow disadvantages a student as to grade, credit, or educational opportunity is presumptively retaliating and the burden is on the school district to prove that what occurred was not retaliation. These presumptions are not easily overcome." Retaliation could also take the form of school officials allowing other students to verbally and otherwise harass a student for filing a complaint.

Other Federal Options

Recall that the Supreme Court decision in the Fitzgerald v. Barnstable (2009) case specifically allowed students to pursue legal action against schools and individuals using federal statutes, other than Title IX. Given the difficult challenges of proving a Title IX case and the inability to sue individual teachers and administrators, attorneys for many student victims have filed federal lawsuits under the provisions using one of the following three options: (1) 42 U.S.C. §1983 Civil Action for Deprivation of Rights, (2) the Equal Protection Clause of the 14th Amendment to the Constitution, and (3) 18 U.S.C. § 241 Conspiracy Against Rights. It is important to note that, if applicable, 42 U.S.C § 1983 allows students to sue individual teachers, school employees, or administrators, and hold them personally accountable for their conduct.

As I mentioned at the beginning of this chapter, it is critical to secure the services of a competent, experienced attorney. This person would be in a position to advise you of the best course of legal action, given the various federal options.

STATE CIVIL AND CRIMINAL LEGAL ACTION

Every state has its own unique set of civil and criminal statutes. While all states have basic laws covering civil rights and criminal offenses, beyond that, there is incredible variety in legal codes. I will briefly discuss potential civil actions that a student victim of sexual abuse/harassment could initiate and then consider potential criminal charges.

Potential Civil Actions

If the sexual abuser/harasser is a school employee, there are several potential state civil actions that could be initiated against the school and its administrators. They include:

(1) negligent hiring of the sexual abuser/harasser, without adequate evaluation of his/her past record of sexual misconduct or convictions,
(2) negligent retention of the sexual abuser/harasser, when his/her past misconduct should reasonably have resulted in termination, and
(3) negligent supervision of the sexual abuser/harasser.

If a school has unknowingly hired a teacher/employee with a prior record of sexual misconduct, but who nevertheless had positive letters of recommendation from previous employers, civil legal action could potentially be taken against the administrators who provided the positive letters of reference. Possible civil charges in these situations could include:

(1) fraudulently misrepresenting or concealing the true credentials of a teacher/employee, with a known record of sexual misconduct and foreseeable likelihood of future harm,
(2) negligent misrepresentation of the actual credentials of a teacher/employee with a known record of sexual conduct and foreseeable likelihood of future harm, and
(3) negligent entrustment of a teacher/employee with a known record of sexual misconduct to another school district where there is a tangible risk of future harm.

In a recent case in California, school district officials who gave positive, unconditional recommendations about a former employee, despite their knowledge of the employee's past sexual misconduct, were charged with fraud and negligent misrepresentation.

Regardless of whether the abuser/harasser is a school employee or student, here are other potential civil actions that could be initiated:

(1) intentional infliction of emotional distress for continuous, severe, pervasive, or outrageous conduct, or an ineffective response by a school to a student's complaint about on-going harassment,
(2) invasion of privacy if the abuser/harasser continually calls, texts, and/or inquires about sexual matters, and
(3) defamation, if the abuser/harasser initiates rumors about a student's sexual activities.

Recognizing the amazing variation in state laws governing these matters, Thompson's Educator's Guide to Controlling Sexual Harassment (2012, p. 77), lists the following unique possibility for state civil action:

"Institutions may be vulnerable to suits for breach of contract stemming from the Title IX requirements that they must publish a notice stating that they do not discriminate. Such a notice might be construed as creating a contractual obligation between students or employees and the institution, so that a student or employee who did not obtain relief when he or she complained might be able to sue for breach of contract."

Criminal Charges

In all 50 states, any sexual interaction between an adult and a child/minor/under-age person is considered unlawful conduct and criminal charges should be filed. If the abuser is also a child/minor/under-age person, sexual misconduct should be referred to juvenile court authorities.

It is important to note that all 50 states have laws stipulating that educators have a personal responsibility to report suspected (a reasonable suspicion) child abuse of any kind to law enforcement authorities. Unfortunately, when the sexual abuser is a fellow educator, teachers, administrators, union officials, and other school employees rarely meet this legal responsibility. In my opinion, this enabling, aiding, and abetting of child sexual abuse should result in criminal charges.

When child sexual abuse is reported, predators can be charged with a variety of crimes, depending upon the nature of their abusive conduct and the state in which the abuse took place. Below is a list of some of the more common criminal charges filed in child sexual abuse cases, along with definitions adapted from Barron's Law Dictionary, Black's Law Dictionary, and other sources:

Rape—"The penetration, no matter how slight, of the vagina or anus with any body part or object, or oral penetration by a sex organ of another person, without the consent of the victim." (new, expanded definition by the U.S. Department of Justice)

Sodomy—Oral or anal copulation, especially between individuals of the same sex

Statutory Rape—Unlawful intercourse with a person under the age of consent (determined by state law)

Carnal Knowledge—The slightest penetration of the female sexual organ by the male sexual organ

Sexual Exploitation—The use of a child in pornography or other sexually manipulative activity that has already caused or could cause serious emotional damage

Sexual Contact—Intentional touching or contact with the intimate parts of another person's body for the purpose of sexual gratification for the abuser or humiliation/degradation of the victim

Assault—A threat or attempt to forcefully inflict bodily harm on a victim, creating the apprehension that injury is imminent

Battery—The use of physical force to inflict bodily harm on a victim

Stalking—Repeatedly following a person in such a way as to alarm the victim and instill fear of harm

Cyberstalking—Repeated use of the Internet or e-mail to threaten, harass, or embarrass the victim

Child Endangerment—Placing a child in a location or position that exposes him/her to danger or injury

Criminal Confinement/False Imprisonment—restraining or confining someone against her/his will while engaging in sexual abuse/harassment

I am particularly encouraged by recent legal actions initiated by prosecutors around the country to hold supervisors criminally responsible for failing to stop continuing child abuse by teachers or coaches whom they supervise. In my opinion, these supervisors should certainly face criminal charges because they are enabling teachers/coaches to engage in the criminal sexual abuse of children. If this practice becomes more widespread, the incidence of educator sexual abuse of students should drop dramatically.

Two examples will illustrate this newfound aggressiveness on the part of prosecutors.

"Last fall, a superintendent in a small-town district in upstate New York was indicted by a grand jury, charged with a misdemeanor criminal charge and placed on administrative leave by the board of education for allegedly not doing enough to protect several young girls in his district from an elementary school art teacher.

The indictment came about after the teacher was arrested on charges of touching the genitalia, backs and legs of elementary school girls. More than a dozen elementary school girls from grades one through six came forward during an investigation by local police into the alleged sexual abuse by the 37-year-old teacher. Members of the community told the news media they had heard the art teacher had been doing this for years, so they were not surprised the superintendent was indicted for his alleged failure to address the child sexual abuse allegations.

The teacher was allowed to continue his classroom duties for 10 months after the first report of abuse. He was removed only upon his arrest. Where was the superintendent in all of this?"

("Superintendent Accountability for Employees' Abuse", The School Administrator, April 2012, the American Association of School Administrators)

"A judge has upheld charges against two LaPorte school officials who could go to jail on allegations they helped cover up a sexual relationship between a now-former volleyball coach and player. Former LaPorte High School junior varsity assistant

volleyball coach Robert Ashcroft, 46, is presently serving a 21-year prison sentence on convictions of felony sexual misconduct. Ashcroft and the girl met when she was 14, and in 2007, when she was 15, began having sex in a relationship that lasted for more than a year.

Prosecutors allege that Gilliland, the high school athletic director, lied to officers looking into the relationship between Ashcraft and the girl and that Lebo, the girls' high school head volleyball coach, did not come forward because of fears of losing her job.

The defendants are accused of having reason to believe abuse or neglect against the female player was occurring and not reporting it to law enforcement or child protective services between August 2007 and October 2008.

Specifically, prosecutors pointed to testimony from state police detective Mike Robinson, who said parents, before law enforcement became involved, had reported to Gilliland questionable activities between Ashcraft and the girl.

'All of these instances were documented by Gilliland as inappropriate behavior in his own words,' Robinson said in his written findings presented in court.

Prosecutors also pointed out that in Ashcraft's personnel file, Lebo revealed witnessing instances that included Ashcraft at a volleyball tournament leaning between the legs of the girl and on a bus ride putting his arm around the girl and sharing food.

It's also alleged that Lebo told her players to keep quiet about any rumors between Ashcraft and one of her players, prosecutors said.

Gilliland and Lebo are each charged with two counts of Class B misdemeanor failure of duty to report and remain free on bond awaiting the outcome of the case."
(www.articles.wsbt.com/2012-02-09)

As you can see, there are many different criminal charges that can be brought against a child sexual abuser.

CONCLUSIONS

The legal issues related to sexual abuse/harassment of students are numerous and complicated. Often times, you are confronted with multiple options for taking action against the abuser, enabling administrators, and the school itself. As I stated in the introduction to this chapter, the best advice I can give you is to find a competent attorney, with experience in these matters, to counsel you about recommended legal options, given the facts in your case and the state you live in.

Hopefully, the information in this chapter will help you to: (1) better understand the legal issues surrounding the sexual abuse/harassment of students and (2) make more informed decisions about your legal options. I encourage you to share this information with your attorney and encourage her/him to be as creative and aggressive as possible in representing you and your child.

CHAPTER 6

FILING A COMPLAINT

In the case discussed at the beginning of Chapter 5, involving the 13-year-old girl and 18-year-old male star athlete, the consequences for filing the complaint were devastating to the girl and her family. Although the boy "admitted to the {sexual} assault during a phone conversation recorded by the Sheriff's Department", Courthouse News Service reported that the girl and her family were: "stalked, persecuted, and harassed", "slandered", "intimidated", "threatened", "run off the road", and "cursed at by students, school employees, and members of the community." "All of this forced the family to move to another school district for their own protection." Courthouse News Service, August 26, 2011 (www.courthousenews.com)

INTRODUCTION

Filing a complaint against someone who has sexually abused/harassed your daughter or son is a natural response on the part of any parent. As with any action you undertake, there are positives and negatives.

In this chapter, I will begin with a discussion of the major potential advantages and disadvantages of filing a complaint. I will then discuss a set of prerequisites that should be met before filing a complaint. Finally, I will discuss the pros and cons associated with five specific complaint filing options. My hope is that this information will help you make better decisions about complaint filing options for you and your family.

ADVANTAGES OF COMPLAINT FILING

There are several potential advantages of filing a complaint against anyone who has sexually abused/harassed your daughter or son. They include: (1) justice for your child, (2) compensation for pain and suffering, (3) helping to stop the menace of child sexual abuse/harassment, and (4) setting a good example for your child. I'll talk about each one of these.

Justice for Your Child By filing a complaint against someone who sexually abused/harassed your child, you are setting in motion a process to seek justice for the wrong(s) that was committed. While there is no guarantee of success, filing a complaint represents an attempt to hold the perpetrator(s) responsible for his/her offenses and seek appropriate punishments. Thus, complaint filing is a fundamental first step in the justice process. From my perspective, if colluding school administrators have enabled a child sexual predator to abuse/harass my child, I want all of the guilty parties prosecuted criminally and civilly to the maximum extent of the law.

Compensation for Pain and Suffering As discussed in Chapter 1, sexual abuse/harassment can have devastating, lifelong consequences for victims and their families. These consequences can include physical/medical problems, psychological disorders, behavioral and school-related problems, and in extreme cases, suicide.   In Chapter 9, I will discuss the process of recovering from sexual abuse/harassment. As you might suspect, it is often lengthy (even life-long) and can be very expensive.

Filing civil complaints against the predator, colluding administrators, and the school district is the only way to obtain compensation for past and future pain and suffering inflicted upon your child and family. Again, while there is no guarantee of success, without filing complaints there is zero probability of securing compensation. In my opinion, if colluding school administrators have enabled someone to sexually abuse/harass my child, I absolutely want all of the individuals and the school system held accountable financially for the pain and suffering inflicted.

Helping to Stop Child Sexual Abuse/Harassment Think about it – if no one ever files a complaint of child sexual abuse/harassment against predators, colluding administrators, or enabling school districts, the abuse will never stop. Without any threat of accountability or punishment, predators would be encouraged to continue and expand their brazen pursuit of child victims, and sexual abuse/harassment of K-12 students would increase dramatically. We need more brave women and men, and girls and boys to file complaints about sexual abusers/harassers. The predators, colluding administrators, and enabling schools need to know that parents will no longer tolerate the abuse/harassment of their children and will hold all guilty parties fully accountable. Only in this manner will we be successful in stopping this horrible problem.

Setting a Good Example for Your Child Filing a complaint on behalf of your child provides a good example for her/him in two major ways. First, you are clearly demonstrating your love and concern for her/his welfare and willingness to fight to protect your child. This can be very validating and reassuring for a young person.

Second, filing a complaint shows your child how to deal with life's injustices—not by ignoring them or "running away", but by aggressively confronting them head-on using established grievance systems and the courts to seek justice. Filing a complaint shows your child that it is important to "stick up for oneself" and not passively allow abuse to continue and abusers to act with impunity. From my perspective, showing your child how to deal with threats to her/his welfare is a critically important lesson to learn.

Disadvantages of Complaint Filing

Unfortunately, there are multiple, powerful potential disadvantages associated with filing a complaint for sexual abuse/harassment. Taken together, these disadvantages function as a potent deterrent to complaint filing and help explain why so few students and their parents do so.

Recall the information cited in Chapter 1 about children's pronounced tendency not to report sexual abuse/harassment. The 2004 Department of Education report stated (p. 34):

"Several studies estimate that only about <u>6 percent</u> [emphasis added] of all children report sexual abuse by an adult to someone who can do something about it. The other 94 percent do not tell anyone or talk only to a friend (and they swear their friend to secrecy)."

Also noted is the fact that few students or families report sexual abuse incidents involving educators to law enforcement authorities.

Among the major potential disadvantages to complaint filing are: (1) perceived negative outcomes for students, (2) retaliation, (3) re-injury in the complaint resolution process, (4) disrupted recovery process, (5) civil lawsuit against you by the harasser, (6) time consuming, (7) public scrutiny, (8) stressful, and (9) financially expensive.

1. <u>Perceived Negative Outcomes by Student Victims</u> The overwhelming majority (94%) of children don't report sexual abuse for several powerful reasons, including (1) fear of punishment by parents or the school, (2) fear of threatened reprisal from the abuser, (3) concern about not being believed, and (4) concern about ill-treatment, ridicule, or rejection by other students. As the Department of Education report (2004, p. 34) noted, "When alleged misconduct [by educators] is reported, the majority of complaints are ignored or disbelieved." Thus, the concerns that children have are clearly well-founded.

2. <u>Retaliation</u> Filing a sexual abuse/harassment complaint against a popular student or teacher can often result in a tidal wave of criticism, threats, intimidation, slander, and harassment, as dramatically shown in the case at the beginning of this chapter. If your child has already been injured by the sexual predator(s), this additional persecution can be absolutely overwhelming.

How outrageous is this? Your child has been victimized by an abusive predator, did nothing wrong, and is simply seeking justice by filing a complaint. In spite of this reality, your child and your family may be cast as the villains in the situation and persecuted for filing a complaint. This is clearly a case of "adding insult to injury".

As parents, you need to think long and hard about this possibility and whether filing a complaint is in the best interest of your child and your family. In other words, how much more can your daughter or son take? If you decide to proceed, you should anticipate retaliation and prepare yourself, your child, and your family to deal with it.

As mentioned in Chapter 5, retaliation against someone for filing a sexual abuse/harassment complaint is unlawful. Thus, civil legal action can be taken against the perpetrators.

3. <u>Reinjury in the Complaint Resolution Process.</u> Sadly, the process of resolving or responding to complaints of sexual abuse/harassment can often result in re-injury to your child. She/he could be compelled to recount what happened or testify repeatedly throughout the process. Each time this happens, your daughter/son resuffers the original trauma. Many child victims simply want the abuse to stop and never want to talk about it again, because they relive the pain.

The authors of <u>Teachers That {Who} Sexually Abuse Students</u> (1999, p. 79) made the following important points about this issue:

"Children who become part of a trial as witnesses may be further victimized by participation in the legal proceedings. For that reason, many parents have chosen to avoid court in order to protect children who have already suffered abuse. In the process, the perpetrator gains an advantage. I do believe though that this process can further abuse a child. For example, the <u>seven years</u> {emphasis added} that the McMartin Preschool students were involved in legal proceedings was probably not to their benefit."

My experience has been that oftentimes unscrupulous predators, colluding administrators, and attorneys who represent them use this fear of revictimization in the legal process to discourage parents from filing lawsuits in the first place or encourage them to drop a lawsuit once filed. Seeing your injured child hurt again is every parent's worst nightmare. Clearly, significant changes are needed in our legal system to protect child victims from being reinjured.

4. <u>Disrupted Recovery Process</u> As the example above states, the legal process in the case cited took <u>seven years</u> to be resolved. Thus, it was impossible during this period for the child victims and their families to fully recover from the abuse, get some measure of closure as to what happened to them, and move on with their lives. As long as the revictimization continues, the recovery process will be thwarted. This is a very serious matter that parents need to consider, in collaboration with the mental health professional treating their child and family. The last thing you want to do is pursue long drawn-out legal action, while seeing your child continue to suffer and never recover.

In a case that I am personally familiar with, an 18-year-old female student was sexually assaulted by a teacher who had asked her to stop by his home to pick-up a letter of recommendation. The family filed a complaint with the school, and the teacher argued that the girl had intended to seduce him in exchange for the letter.

Outraged, the family then filed a civil lawsuit against the school and teacher. The soulless attorney for the school scheduled a deposition (sworn testimony in response to questions asked) for the girl. In the room were the girl, her parents, her attorney, the school attorney, and a court reporter.

The questioning quickly became insulting and demeaning. The school attorney asked the following outrageous question: Isn't your attempted sexual seduction of the teacher consistent with your slut-like behavior throughout high school? The girl burst into tears. Her father exploded and started across the table after the school attorney. Thankfully, her mother and attorney were able to restrain him.

A break was called to allow everyone to compose themselves. After discussing what had just happened, the girl's parents decided to drop the lawsuit immediately and go home. They could not stand the thought of putting their daugh-

ter through any more pain like this. Sadly, the school's "attack-dog" tactics had worked and the girl continues to struggle in her recovery to this day.

5. <u>Civil Lawsuit Against You by the Predator</u> Some sexual predators attempt to intimidate victims and their families and discourage them from filing a complaint by threatening a civil lawsuit. They argue that their "good" reputation must be protected from defamation, which involves communicating <u>inaccurate</u> negative information verbally (slander) or in writing (libel).

Thus, it is important for you to be very careful about what you say or write about the alleged predator. Once again, the advice of a competent, experienced attorney can be invaluable in avoiding these problems. If all of your statements about the alleged abuser are true, this constitutes a complete and valid defense against charges of slander or libel.

Even if everything you say or write is completely truthful, a devilish sexual predator can still sue you for libel and slander, necessitating that you hire an attorney to defend yourself. In fact, this happened to me many years ago. I filed a complaint against a faculty member at my school for sexual misconduct with a student. After he confessed, I pressed the administration for an appropriate punishment but he only received a suspension with full pay for one semester, in other words, a paid 3 1/2 month vacation.

In an attempt to retaliate against me and discourage anyone from ever filing a complaint against him in the future, he sued me for libel and slander. Needless to say, I was a bit upset at this ridiculous lawsuit and searched for the most aggressive attorney in town.

Thankfully, I found him. After describing my situation, I requested that he mount an aggressive "no holds barred" defense. He responded that the best defense is a good offense and advised that I counter-sue and put pressure on the predator. This kind of attacking style was just what I was looking for. We counter-sued and the predator quickly agreed to mutually drop both lawsuits. Although victorious in the end, I still had to pay $5,000.00 in legal fees.

6. <u>Time Consuming</u> Complaints of child sexual abuse/ harassment are rarely resolved in a timely manner. Investigating and processing your complaint through the school, Office for Civil Rights, criminal courts, or civil courts can take anywhere from several months to several years, as noted in the case discussed earlier in this chapter. The activities required in pursuing a complaint are very time consuming. They include: (1) completing documents, (2) obtaining records, (3) meeting with school, government agency, or police officials, (4) finding an attorney, (5) meeting with your attorney, (6) reviewing documents, (7) preparing for hearings, (8) attending hearings, and (9) traveling to and from the required meetings and hearings. These additional demands on your time can be overwhelming and seemingly endless.

   My experience has been that schools, predators, and their attorneys will do everything possible, and more, to delay resolution of the case, and cause more work and hassle for you. Their goal of course is to frustrate you and make everything more time consuming and expensive, so that you drop the case.

7. <u>Public Scrutiny</u>Once the media become aware of your complaint, everyone in your family could face intense public attention and scrutiny, especially your child. Accusations of child sexual abuse/harassment are deemed very newsworthy by the media and thus will likely result in one or more (or even a series) of articles about your child and her/his experiences at school.

8. <u>Stressful</u> Even thinking about filing a complaint is stressful for most parents. Certainly the steps involved in filing any complaint alleging sexual abuse/harassment of your child are incredibly stressful. Once the stress begins, it continues unabated until your complaint is finally resolved, which could take years. It will affect everyone in your family, although you, your spouse, and your child will be most seriously impacted.

9. <u>Financially Expensive</u> In addition to the lost time from work, due to attending required complaint-related meetings/hearings, there

are potentially substantial financial expenses involved in filing a complaint on behalf of your daughter or son. For example, consulting with a competent, experienced attorney about your filing options will require you to pay her/his hourly rate which could be $300.00 or more.

If you decide to pursue a civil lawsuit against the school, predator(s), and/or enabling administrator in order to recover financial damages for the harm done to your child, some law firms will take your case on a contingent-fee basis. This means that you only pay them (typically 40% of the total damage award) if you win the case. However, you are still obligated to pay any expenses related to your case. This could include expert witness costs to document the harm done to your child and estimate the damages owed or to document the ineffective actions of the school to correct the sexual abuse/harassment. A competent, experienced expert witness who produces a report of findings and testifies on your behalf can easily cost $20,000.00 or more.

Finally, as mentioned above, you need to be prepared to hire an attorney if the predator files a civil lawsuit for libel or slander against you. All of this can add-up quickly and result in huge expenses.

PREREQUISITES FOR FILING A COMPLAINT

Seven prerequisites need to be met before you file a complaint. I will briefly discuss each one: (1) courage, (2) perseverance, (3) social and emotional support, (4) stress management, (5) evidence, (6) legal advice, and (7) financial resources.

1. <u>Courage</u> As presented above, there are multiple significant potential risks/disadvantages associated with filing a complaint. Thus, it takes a great deal of courage to face these challenges and move forward in spite of them.

2. <u>Perseverance</u> Complaints are rarely resolved in a timely manner. Therefore, you should be prepared for a long drawn-out process that will require patience and perseverance in order to prevail.
3. <u>Social and Emotional Support</u> There is no question that filing a complaint will result in significant stress for you, your child, and your entire family. In order to cope with these demands, it is essential that social and emotional support be available to everyone in the family. Trusted family members, clergy, friends, and counselors can all serve this critical function.
4. <u>Stress Management</u> In order to deal with the significant stress associated with filing a complaint for you, your child, and other family members, it is important that everyone be familiar with stress management techniques and how to effectively use them. With this in mind, I have a free online tutorial on managing stress, based upon over 30 years of teaching, training, and researching on the topic. It is available at http://lifestress.indiana.edu, by clicking on "About Coping with Stress". All of the techniques discussed can be equally useful to adults and children.
5. <u>Evidence</u> Without solid evidence, you will not be able to document or support your complaint. Chapter 7 discusses the topic of evidence in great detail. Before filing a complaint you should be confident that you have the evidence necessary to prove your case.
6. <u>Legal Advice</u> Complaints alleging sexual abuse/harassment of children inevitably involve important legal issues – both criminal and civil. Consequently, it is critical to find a competent, experienced attorney to advise you throughout this process. As mentioned in Chapter 5, the National Crime Victim Bar Association (202-467-8716) can be very helpful in making referrals to local attorneys with experience in child sexual abuse cases.
7. <u>Financial Resources</u> If you choose to file a civil complaint in court, you may be faced with substantial bills for legal and related (i.e., expert witness) services. You also need to be prepared to defend yourself against potential civil lawsuits filed against you by the accused abuser(s). Ideally, before filing, you should insure that sufficient financial resources are available to cover these expenses. You can always consider asking family, friends, coworkers, and even internet donors to help you with legal fees.

COMPLAINT FILING OPTIONS

If your daughter or son has been a victim of sexual abuse/harassment at school, you have a number of different complaint filing options. They include: (1) a school complaint, (2) a complaint with the office for Civil Rights (OCR) of the U.S. Department of Education, (3) a criminal complaint, (4) a civil lawsuit complaint, or a (5) media complaint. For each of these options, I will briefly describe the steps involved, followed by a discussion of the major pros and cons.

1. <u>School Complaint</u>

This option entails taking your complaint directly to school officials. I certainly recommend that the complaint be in writing and addressed to: (1) the school system's designated Title IX Coordinator, if there is one, (2) the school system superintendent, and (3) the president of the school board. Sending the same written complaint to multiple school officials substantially reduces the likelihood that they will contend your complaint was never received.

I also recommend that you send your written complaint by email and registered mail. Keep copies of all emails sent to and received from the school as documentation of what you did and when you did it. The goal is to clearly document that your complaint was received by senior school officials with the authority to address the issues raised. In order to secure your rights under Title IX (as discussed in Chapter 5), it is critical that you file your complaint alleging sexual abuse/harassment at school within 180 days of the date of the incident. Complying with this deadline will enable you to file a complaint with the Office for Civil Rights (OCR) or file a civil lawsuit under Title IX against the school, if you so choose.

Pros and Con

The major pros and cons associated with filing a complaint through the school include the following:

Pros

1. If filed with a senior school official, this satisfies the Supreme Court Title IX requirement for notification of an administrator with the authority to address issues raised,
2. If filed within 180 days of the incident, this satisfies the OCR regulations concerning the statute of limitations and allows you to file complaints with the OCR or file a Title IX civil lawsuit, and
3. Gives the school and opportunity to investigate and correct the problem.

Cons

1. High likelihood that your complaint will be ignored,
2. If investigated, strong probability that the investigator will be an untrained school employee, thus precluding a competent, independent, unbiased investigation,
3. Little likelihood that the abuser(s) or enabling administrators will receive appropriate discipline or that effective corrective/protective actions will be taken,
4. No possibility of collecting financial compensation for the harm done, and
5. High probability of retaliation, intimidation, and harassment for filing the complaint.

2. <u>Office for Civil Rights (OCR) Complaint</u>

As discussed in Chapter 5, the OCR is the enforcement agency for Title IX in the Department of Education. If you believe your daughter or son has been sexually abused/harassed at school, you (as the parent or legal guardian) can file a complaint with the OCR on behalf of your child. An online version of the complaint form, which can then be submitted electronically, is available at www2.ed.gov/about/offices/list/ocr/complaintintro.html. Complaints to the OCR should be filed within 180 days of the alleged violation of Title IX. However, if you have already filed a complaint directly with the school, the OCR requires that you await a final report from the school on your complaint, before filing with them. It is important to note that you have 60 days from the date of the school's final report to file a complaint with the OCR.

An investigation of your complaint will be conducted by a trained OCR professional. If your allegations of sexual abuse/harassment are supported, the OCR will attempt to negotiate a voluntary settlement. If the offending school refuses to cooperate, the OCR will issue a Letter of Finding stating the conclusions of its investigation. If the noncompliant school continues to refuse to negotiate a resolution, the OCR will issue a Letter of Impending Enforcement Action, and again attempt a voluntary resolution. If unsuccessful, the OCR "will either initiate administrative enforcement proceedings to suspend, terminate, or refuse to grant or continue Federal financial assistance to the recipient, or will refer the case to the Department of Justice. OCR may also move immediately to defer any new or additional Federal financial assistance to the institution." (Page 9 of 11, U.S. Department of Education, Office for Civil Rights Discrimination Complaint Form, Consent Form, and Complaint Processing Procedures)

Unfortunately, as I mentioned in Chapter 5, an OCR staff attorney confirmed for me that no school has ever been denied federal funding for a sexual abuse/harassment violation of Title IX. Thus, this threat is ignored by schools which are essentially free to disregard OCR findings, without fear of punishment.

This lack of enforcement authority is likely a major reason for the near complete underutilization of the OCR by K-12 students. Recall from Chapter 5 that of the 69 sexual harassment complaints filed with the OCR in FY 2008 (the most recent year available), none were filed by K-12 students.

Pros and Cons

Among the most important pros and cons of filing a complaint with the OCR are:

Pros

1. Due to the OCR's notification of senior school administrators when a complaint is received about their institution, this satisfies the

Supreme Court Title IX requirement to file complaints with school officials who have the authority to address issues raised,
2. If filed first with the OCR within 180 days of the incident or within 60 days of the issuance of a school's report on your complaint, this satisfies the OCR regulation concerning the statute of limitations and also allows you to file a Title IX civil lawsuit,
3. A professional, unbiased investigation of your complaint,
4. An independent decision about guilt or innocence will be made by a trained professional unaffiliated with the school,
5. A favorable report of findings can be very embarrassing to the school and its leaders, and
6. A favorable report of findings could help document criminal and/or civil charges against the predator(s), enabling administrators, and school.

Cons

1. Due to limited staffing and resources, complaint processing can be very slow, often taking several months or longer,
2. For the reasons discussed above, there is little likelihood that the school or sexual predator will face punishment as a result of your complaint,
3. No possibility of collecting financial compensation, and
4. High probability of retaliation, intimidation, and harassment for filing the complaint.

3. <u>Criminal Complaint</u>

Filing a criminal complaint involves contacting law enforcement authorities (i.e. city, county, state police) and providing a description of the alleged unlawful conduct, along with any potential evidence you have. Useful resources and general advice for crime victims and their families is available from The National Center for Victims of Crime at www.victimsofcrime.org. This process typically requires completing and signing a report that summarizes what allegedly happened.

Police officers will then conduct a preliminary investigation of the alleged criminal conduct. Results of this investigation and any evidence collected will be submitted to the appropriate prosecutor's office, where a decision will be made about what, if any, criminal charges will be brought, and if so, specifically what charges. Depending upon the nature of exactly what happened to your child and the state in which it happened, several potential criminal charges could be filed. A long list of these criminal charges was provided in Chapter 5. Suffice it to say that any sexual conduct between an adult and child constitutes criminal behavior. The prosecutor will determine which of the possible charges will be brought against your child's abuser/harasser, and if appropriate, set a tentative trial date.

Pros and Cons

The pros and cons of filing a criminal complaint with law enforcement authorities include the following:

Pros

1. A professional, unbiased investigation of your complaint by a trained law enforcement officer,
2. An independent decision about guilt will be made by a judge or jury,
3. The possibility of justice and appropriate criminal punishment for the sexual predator(s) and enabling administrators, and
4. The opportunity to send a powerful message to the individual sexual predator(s) and enabling administrators (and anyone in these two categories at other schools) that they will be held criminally accountable for what they have done.

Cons

1. No control over whether the prosecutor decides to file criminal charges based upon the evidence presented,
2. A higher, more difficult evidence standard for a guilty verdict – "beyond a reasonable doubt",

3. With over-crowded court systems throughout the country, it could take anywhere from several months to years for a final outcome, especially if appeals are involved,
4. The possibility of a "plea bargain" by the predator to lesser charges that result in little or no incarceration time,
5. Your child is subjected to the stresses and trauma associated with our legal system, often revictimizing her/him, especially during questioning by opposing attorneys,
6. Your child's recovery from the abuse suffered is disrupted and lengthened,
7. No possibility of collecting financial compensation,
8. High probability of retaliation, intimidation, and harassment for filing the complaint, and
9. Will likely result in media attention and public scrutiny.

4. Civil Lawsuit

In order to file a civil lawsuit against the sexual predator(s), school, and individual enabling administrators, you will need to find and hire a competent, experienced attorney. As discussed in Chapter 5, there are a wide variety of possible civil charges that can be filed in sexual abuse/harassment cases, depending upon exactly what happened and in which state it occurred.

Recall also from Chapter 5, that some types of civil charges only allow you to file against the school and not the individual perpetrators or administrators—Title IX lawsuits are in this category. If you wish to file charges against the individuals involved, you and your attorney will need to consider other federal or state statutes. I would encourage you and your attorney to file as many charges as are legally possible against the school, individual perpetrators, and individual enabling/incompetent administrators.

Once civil charges are filed, a tentative trial date will be set, along with a time period for discovery. The discovery process allows both sides to request and collect relevant information needed for trial.

Pros and Cons

The pros and cons associated with filing a civil lawsuit include:

Pros

1. You and your attorney are in control of what civil charges are filed and when,
2. A lower, more easily achieved evidence standard for a guilty verdict – "more likely than not",
3. The possibility of justice in the form of financial penalties for the sexual predator(s) and enabling administrators,
4. The opportunity to send a clear message to the individual sexual predator(s) and enabling administrators (and anyone in these two categories at other schools) that they will be held financially accountable for the damage they have caused,
5. The possibility of receiving financial compensation for the damages done to your child and family,
6. The possibility of court-ordered changes in school policies and practices to more effectively prevent and correct sexual abuse/harassment, and
7. The possibility of an out-of-court settlement to avoid the embarrassment and substantial additional cost of having a public trial.

Cons

1. With over-crowded court systems throughout the country, it could take anywhere from several months to years for a final outcome, especially if appeals are involved,
2. Your child is subjected to the stresses and trauma associated with our legal system, often revictimizing her/him, especially during questioning by opposing attorneys,
3. Your child's recovery from the abuse suffered is disrupted and lengthened,
4. Can be very expensive (attorney fees, expert witness costs) with no hope of recovering money spent if you lose the case,
5. Could result in media attention and public scrutiny, and
6. High probability of retaliation, intimidation, and harassment for filing the lawsuit.

5. Media Complaint

This approach simply involves contacting a local newspaper, radio station, or television station to share your complaint. In the aftermath of the horrible Sandusky scandal at Penn State, news media are especially interested in stories documenting child sexual abuse. Typically a reporter will be assigned to collect details about the nature of your child's abuse, the alleged abuser, and the school in which it occurred. If the appropriate news editor approves, the story or stories will appear in the near future. Remember my cautions earlier about possible slander charges brought by an alleged abuser/harasser against you for something you said about him.

Pros and Cons

Included among the major pros and cons of filing a media complaint are:

Pros

1. Quickly bring attention to your child's case,
2. May motivate the school system, predator(s), and or enabling administrators to quickly settle your case and make requested improvements in institutional policies and practices , and
3. Increase public pressure on the prosecutor's office to file criminal charges against the predator(s) and school administrators.

Cons

1. Will result in immediate, potentially intense public attention and scrutiny,
2. Public scrutiny and media attention could revictimize your child,
3. Public scrutiny and media attention could disrupt and lengthen your child's recovery, and
4. High probability of retaliation, intimidation, and harassment for going to the press.

In a case that I am personally familiar with, three girls and their parents filed sexual harassment complaints against several teachers and school employees. After being told it would take several months to investigate and resolve the complaints, the parents scheduled a joint meeting with the senior school administrator to present him with an ultimatum: Complete the investigations, take appropriate disciplinary/corrective action, initiate a list of preventive actions including training all employees and students within one month, or the parents and students would go to the local media. It is important to note that their demands did not include any financial compensation for damages.

Schools are not known for being run efficiently or taking any action in a timely manner. However, confronted with the looming possibility of three families complaining to the press and the inevitable negative publicity for the school and its employees, the administration did manage to satisfactorily meet the parent's demands and avert the impending public relations disaster.

CONCLUSIONS

The decision about whether or not to file a sexual abuse/harassment complaint on behalf of your child is one of the most important and difficult you will ever make. The consequences of your decision will have a huge impact on your child and your entire family.

As discussed in this chapter, there are both significant advantages and disadvantages to complaint filing. You also have multiple available options, each with its own pros and cons.

I hope the information I have provided will help you in making these critical decisions. I highly recommend seeking the advice of a competent, experienced attorney before you make a final decision.

Remember, the health and well-being of your child must be protected, no matter what you decide to do. Good luck in doing what is best for your child and family.

CHAPTER 7

COLLECTING EVIDENCE TO PROVE YOUR CASE

*I*n a recent case in Texas, allegations that a high school teacher sexually assaulted one of his female students were corroborated by the discovery of 900 sexually explicit calls and texts between the two of them over a period of nine days.

When filing a complaint of sexual abuse/harassment on behalf of your daughter or son, it is extremely important to have solid evidence to support your allegations. A complaint without evidence will be dismissed, as it should be in our judicial system. Charges of sexual abuse/harassment are very serious and thus necessitate careful consideration of how to best document them.

In this chapter, I will briefly review the two different evidence standards in criminal and civil cases. Then I will discuss the types of evidence and various collection strategies. Generally, the stronger your evidence, the better your chances of success.

EVIDENCE STANDARDS

The standards for evidence and proof are different for criminal and civil offenses. To prove criminal charges, the evidence standard is "beyond a reasonable doubt". In other words, if a reasonable doubt can be established or another logical explanation offered, the verdict should be not guilty.

The evidence standard with civil charges is less rigorous – "more likely than not", or 51% likely. Thus, it is much easier to prove civil charges than criminal ones.

A prominent example of the different evidence standards was the O.J. Simpson case. The available evidence resulted in: (1) a not guilty verdict on the criminal charges of murdering his ex-wife and her boyfriend and (2) a guilty verdict on civil claims brought by the boyfriend's father.

TYPES OF EVIDENCE AND COLLECTION STRATEGIES

There are seven types of evidence that you could use to document charges of sexual abuse/harassment. These include:

(1) DNA evidence,
(2) written incident documentation,
(3) written/printed information from the abuser/harasser,
(4) tape recording,
(5) video recording,
(6) witnesses, and
(7) prior victims.

I will briefly discuss each of these, along with potential collection strategies and illustrative cases.

It is important to emphasize that you should consult with law enforcement authorities about evidence collection if you have filed criminal allegations, and with your attorney if you have filed a civil suit. These professionals are best positioned to provide you with appropriate advice, given the nature of your complaint.

1. DNA Evidence

If your child has been brazenly victimized by a sexual assault, it is essential that you immediately report the attack to law enforcement authorities, do not let your child shower or use the restroom as that could destroy potential evidence, take your child to a local hospital for a medical exam, and arrange for mental health counseling. A trained doctor can identify and document the trauma your child has endured, treat the physical injuries, and possibly collect DNA evidence that could be used against the predator. Emergency rooms have specially trained professionals who help your child through the ordeal. Similarly, trained police officers can determine if there are other ways to collect DNA samples from the available evidence.

In cases involving sexual attacks, DNA evidence offers the strongest possible proof against the predator. Thus, seek professional assistance as soon as possible to maximize the likelihood of obtaining this critical evidence.

2. Written Incident Documentation

I highly recommend that you and your child keep detailed written documentation of every incident of sexual abuse/harassment. This information is critical in supporting your allegations against the predator(s).

In my experiences as an expert witness in court and human resource management consultant to companies, I have repeatedly seen the value of detailed written documentation in helping to substantiate sexual abuse/harassment allegations. The lack of accurate incident documentation can seriously undermine your case.

For example, in the absence of written documentation, you and your child might be uncertain as to exactly when abusive/harassing incidents occurred and cite incorrect dates in your complaint. If the abuser/harasser can prove that he was out-of-town (at a professional conference, on vacation, etc.) on the dates in your complaint, your charges could easily be dismissed. Thus, accurate documentation provides the foundation upon which successful complaints are filed.

With this in mind, I have used and recommend a simple, straightforward form to record information about sexually abusive/harassing incidents, ideally as soon as possible after the occurrence. It is contained in Figure 7-1. If you file a criminal complaint with law enforcement authorities, the police will prepare a written report containing information similar to that in the figure.

FIGURE 7-1

SEXUAL ABUSE/HARASSMENT INCIDENT FORM

DATE: _____
TIME INCIDENT OCCURRED: _____
PLACE INCIDENT OCCURRED: _____
NAMES OF OTHER PEOPLE PRESENT: _____

1. Description of Sexual Abuse/Harassment (What specifically did the perpetrator say or do?)

_____
_____
_____
_____
_____

2. In response to the Sexual Abuse/Harassment, what did you say or do?

_____
_____
_____
_____
_____

3. In response to the Sexual Abuse/Harassment, how did you feel?

_____
_____
_____
_____
_____

4.	Did you take any action after the incident? If yes, what action(s) did you take?

_____
_____
_____
_____
_____

5.	Did you talk with anyone after the incident? If yes, with whom did you talk and what was the content of your conversation?

_____
_____
_____
_____
_____

3. Written/Printed Information From the Abuser/Harasser

Handwritten, typed, or electronically transmitted messages from the abuser/harasser to your child can provide powerful evidence to support your complaint. This information can include: (1) signed, handwritten notes or letters, (2) unsigned handwritten notes or letters which require matching with other samples of the abuser's/harasser's writing, (3) email messages from the abuser's/harasser's account, (4) text messages from the abuser's/harasser's number, and (5) messages sent through a social media account.

Two recent cases underscore the value of written/printed messages in documenting charges of sexual abuse/harassment.

According to the Citypages Blogs (www.blogs.citypages.com, 24 Feb 12), a 66-year-old bus driver in Minnesota was charged with second degree sexual assault involving a 15-year-old girl who rode his bus. The girl's mother had discovered a love letter written by the bus driver to her daughter and he later confessed to sexual contact with the girl on two occasions.

A school board in New York recently took disciplinary action against a teacher for sending sexually explicit emails to a female student. The girl's mother's suspicions had been confirmed when she inadvertently discovered the emails and presented them to school authorities.

4. Tape Recording

Tape recording a sexual abuser/harasser while he is engaged in unlawful conduct or talking about past acts can provide virtually indisputable evidence to support your complaint. Before using this approach, be sure to confirm that it is legal in your state.

Writing in <u>Managing Human Resources</u> (2010), Cascio states that federal law permits secret tape recording, as long as one person being taped is aware of it. State laws vary, with at least 11 states requiring that both parties are aware of the taping. The best advice before using a tape recorder is to check with a local attorney or do an online search of your state's laws.

Cascio also notes that companies confronted with tape recordings "quickly settle out of court". That has certainly been my experience with schools as well. Since technology exists to reliably match a person's voice with that on a tape, this type of evidence is nearly impossible to challenge.

There are two ways to collect tape recorded information. The first one involves taping during face-to-face interaction with the abuser/harasser or enabling administrator. A high quality, digital micro-recorder can be purchased from any electronics retailer and easily concealed in your pocket. If you are able to have a private conversation with the abuser/harasser or administrator to discuss incidents involving your child, they will often make statements and admissions that can be used later to support your complaint. Always be sure to make multiple copies of the recording and keep them in separate locations.

Here is how I used this strategy. It involved a mental health medical malpractice/fraud case against someone misrepresenting his credentials and providing services to my son as a Ph.D. clinical psychologist, when he only had a master's degree in school psychology. As is the case with many lawbreakers, this imposter was arrogant and believed he was invincible and above the law. I made an appointment and arrived with a high fidelity microcassette tape recorder hidden in my shirt pocket. I asked him several questions about his credentials, and he bragged that he had fooled the hospital into believing he was a Ph.D., and admitted that he really wasn't qualified to treat my son, but blamed everything on the hospital.

Of course, he had no idea that I was taping him, and it was legal in that state. I took a copy of the ½-hour tape to the county prosecutor, who had been struggling to find solid evidence against this fraud. After listening to the tape, deputies were dispatched to make an arrest and he was successfully prosecuted in court, <u>using his own words as evidence</u>.

The second way to collect tape recorded evidence involves installing special equipment on your home phone (although these are fast becoming extinct due to the proliferation of cell phones) that enables you to record all conversations. Once again, check with your attorney or state statutes to insure this is legal. Use of this equipment would allow you to tape conversations between the abuser/harasser and your child or between you and the abuser/harasser in a manner similar to that described above. These devices are easily available online from major electronic retailers. Alternatively, you could put your phone on speaker mode and then use a recorder to tape the conversation.

Voice mail messages left by the abuser/harasser on any type of phone can also provide solid evidence to support your complaint.

In a recent New York case, parents of a 17-year-old high school girl had complained many times to school officials about a history teacher who they believed was having a sexual relationship with their daughter. No action was taken until the parents discovered a romantic voice message left by the teacher and presented it to school authorities.

5. Video Recording

Video recordings of abusers/harassers provide even stronger evidence than audio tapes to support your complaint. The technology to video tape is readily available in most mobile phones and thus can be easily used to document unlawful conduct. However, the appropriate use of hidden video recorders is a very complicated legal matter and must be discussed with your attorney before proceeding.

The value of video recordings in supporting sexual abuse/harassment allegations is powerfully demonstrated in the following two cases.

A female teacher's aide in Minnesota was sentenced to 90 days in jail for having a sexual relationship with a junior high school male. The boy had made a video of her performing oral sex on him in a car. Police were made aware of the video when the boy shared it online with his friends.

In a recent case in California, a school district had received several complaints from parents about inappropriate sexual relationships between the male coach of the girls' basketball team and several of his players. Although the coach and girls denied that anything was happening, school officials were sufficiently concerned that they hired a private investigator (PI) to monitor the coach's activities outside of school. The PI was able to video tape the coach and one of his female players exiting his condo together, early on a Sunday morning, kissing, and then leaving in separate cars. This compelling evidence resulted in the coach's termination.

6. Witnesses

People who have personally witnessed the sexual abuse/harassment suffered by your child can be invaluable in documenting your complaint, if they agree to testify or provide a sworn statement. Unfortunately, there are two major problems with witnesses.

First, a person who agrees to testify on your behalf can often change her/his mind, sometimes at the last minute. They really don't want to get involved or they fear retaliation and retribution from the abuser/harasser, his supporters, or the school. Sometimes a potential witness's fears are unfounded but in other instances, threats have actually been communicated.

In the days before I was scheduled to testify against my university and a sexually abusive/harassing faculty member, I received a phone call from the law firm representing my school. The attorney told me that it would not be good for my career at Indiana University to testify against the school. This was a blatant instance of attempted witness intimidation. If I had been able to tape the call, I would have pressed charges, but I did not – it would have been her word against mine.

A second problem with witnesses is the research-documented unreliability of their testimony. Recent studies have shown that eye-witness accounts of the same event can vary greatly from person to person, are influenced by a variety of irrelevant factors, and often change over time. These problems are more pronounced if the witnesses are children. Based upon this body of research, opposing expert witnesses can substantially undermine the credibility of eye-witness testimony.

Given these significant problems, I would not recommend that you rely heavily or exclusively on witnesses to prove your allegations. Other forms of evidence are absolutely necessary. Of course, you should also consult with your attorney about this issue.

7. Prior Victims

If your child has been sexually abused/harassed by an educator but there is no corroborating evidence, schools in virtually all cases will automatically believe the teacher, not the student. Without this independent evidence, no action will be taken against the sexual predator.

If you are confronted by this type of situation, I highly recommend that you consider the following strategy. Research confirms that sexual harassers/abusers have typically victimized multiple children over time. Your challenge then is to locate and contact the families of children who previously had contact with the sexual predator (for example, a student in his class, a rider on his bus) and may have also been victimized. School yearbooks can be especially helpful in this regard. Testimony from former students against the accused sexual harasser can be invaluable in substantiating your complaint. If your child was victimized by criminal sexual abuse, law enforcement investigators often utilize a similar strategy in contacting other potential victims.

The criminal case against former Penn State assistant football coach Jerry Sandusky offers a compelling example of the power of prior victims. The initial complaint of sexual abuse by one young man against Sandusky was soon joined by multiple other victims. Eventually, a total of eight brave young men provided graphic, detailed testimony in court about the sexual abuse they suffered as teenagers from Sandusky. After his conviction, jurors commented that the dramatic testimony from the eight victims provided overwhelming evidence of Sandusky's criminal guilt.

CONCLUSIONS

As you can see, there are many ways in which you can collect evidence to support your complaint. Remember, without any evidence, complaints are dismissed as baseless.

The more evidence you can collect, the better your chances are of success. I would encourage you to be meticulous, bold, and aggressive in assembling the strongest evidence possible against your child's abuser/harasser.

Don't forget to seek the advice of law enforcement authorities if you file a criminal complaint and your attorney if you file a civil complaint. Let these trained professionals advise you about the best evidence collecting strategies in your case.

CHAPTER 8

PREPARING AND PROTECTING YOUR CHILD

"*Some offenders will test a child's personal safety awareness and whether or not there is a risk that the child will tell an adult. **Offenders are less likely to victimize a child if they think the child will tell.**"*
Canadian Centre for Child Protection, Child Sexual Abuse It is Your Business (2011, p. 10)

While it is impossible to guarantee that your child will never be sexually abused/harassed at school, there are powerful steps that you can take to dramatically decrease the likelihood of abuse. In this chapter, I will identify and discuss several specific preventive/protective strategies. The challenge for you is to use some combination of these strategies to best prepare and protect your child.

PREVENTIVE/PROTECTIVE STRATEGIES

1. Educate Your Child

It is critically important that your child be taught about essential personal safety topics. While this information should be addressed in schools, too often it is not. Thus, you need to take the responsibility for insuring that your child is properly educated in this area.

Specific topics that should be covered in an age-appropriate manner include:

(1) the names of body parts and clear identification of those that are private,
(2) clear rules for appropriate and inappropriate interaction between children and adults (or older children) that exclude touching private parts,
(3) the importance of being assertive and standing up for yourself when someone attempts inappropriate touching or tries to harm you,
(4) the understanding that some adults in positions of trust, including teachers/educators, may behave inappropriately,
(5) the importance of not keeping secrets about:
   (a) someone taking pictures of you or making videos,
   (b) someone asking you to take your clothes off,
   (c) someone touching your private areas,
   (d) someone asking you to touch their private areas, and
   (e) anything that makes you feel scared, uncomfortable, or upset, and
(6) the need to tell your parent or guardian if someone is treating you in an inappropriate way.

Most parents are ill-equipped to address these topics in a comprehensive and effective manner. Thus, professional assistance is typically needed. While there are many organizations that provide safety advice for children, the best that I have found is a nonprofit Canadian agency.

The Canadian Centre for Child Protection has developed a comprehensive, research-based program to educate children and keep them safe. It is called "Kids in the Know", and information for children, parents, and educators is available online at www.kidsintheknow.ca. I am extremely impressed with the materials developed by this organization and strongly encourage you to personally use the information with your child and recommend it for training purposes in your school system. Excellent educational materials are also available from Yello Dyno, Inc. Their web address is www.yellodyno.com.

2. Never Let Your Child Be Alone with School Employees

Virtually all sexual abuse of K-12 students takes place behind closed doors, in private settings. Thus, to insure that this does not happen to your daughter or son, inform (verbally and in writing) your child's principal and teachers that she/he is not to be alone with any school employee, <u>ever</u>. You can offer to make yourself, your spouse, or another adult family member/friend available to come to school to be present with your child if 1-on-1 interaction with a school employee is needed. Schools should have official policies that prohibit employees from being alone with students, but most don't.

It is important to make sure that your child also understands that he/she is not to be alone with school employees, and reminds them if such a situation begins to develop. If you find out that your child has been alone with a school employee, file a complaint and demand disciplinary action.

3. Understand and Beware of the Grooming Process

Sexual predators typically use a process known as "grooming" to prepare their targets to be abused. Grooming in this context is defined as "deliberate actions undertaken to befriend someone (typically a young person or child) with the intent of preparing them for sexual exploitation".

Steps in the grooming process usually include:
(1) special attention toward the target victim,
(2) special recognition and rewards (verbal praise or small gifts) for the target victim,
(3) special privileges and opportunities (for example, invitations for lunch or outings) for the target victim,
(4) slowly increasing amounts of touching and sexual comments to assess the target victim's response and likelihood of resisting or filing a complaint,
(5) progressive sexual behavior to desensitize the target victim to what is happening, and further test her/his resistance and complaint filing propensity,
(6) acts of sexual exploitation/gratification which can recur for months, and in extreme cases, years, and

(7) emphasis on the victim's mutual responsibility for the sexual activity and continued need for secrecy.

It is critical that both you and your child understand what grooming is and the steps commonly involved. This will enable you to determine if your child has been targeted by a sexual predator. If you sense that grooming is taking place, based upon your own personal observations (see below) or your child's conversations about interaction at school, you should immediately bring your concerns to the attention of the principal and teacher.

Perhaps the grooming-like behavior on the part of the teacher was unintentional or innocent. However, you should clearly state that you don't want your child or any child singled out for special attention. Furthermore, your demands that your child not be alone with the teacher (#2 above) and not be touched by the teacher (#4 below) are non-negotiable. If these demands are not respected, formal written complaints should be filed against the offender.

The key to protecting your child from being groomed by a sexual predator is to stop it before it gets started. This requires monitoring on the part of you and your child, followed by quick corrective action if grooming begins.

4. Never Let Your Child Be Touched By School Employees

As you saw in #3 above, grooming involves progressive touching of a child, ultimately leading to sexual abuse. For this reason, I strongly recommend that you inform (both verbally and in writing) school officials and teachers that your child is not to be touched by any school employee. Of course, this does not apply to someone providing first aid or medical treatment.

Schools should have strict policies about touching students, but most do not. Thus, it is up to you as a concerned parent to insist that your child not be touched. Don't allow sexual predators to use touching as a gateway to abuse your child!

It is important to insure that your child knows she/he is not to be touched by school employees. Violations should be brought to your attention, so that an appropriate complaint can be filed and corrective action initiated.

5. Self-Defense Classes

I am a firm believer in the value of age-appropriate self-defense classes for all school children. This can help enhance their confidence and self-esteem, as well as providing simple techniques to protect themselves from sexual or physical abuse.

In my opinion, self-defense should be a required element in the K-12 curriculum of any school system. Unfortunately, to my knowledge, this is not occurring anywhere in the United States.

Once again, parents must take personal responsibility for obtaining such training. All four of my children have participated in and significantly benefited from basic self-defense training. In each case, I had to search for an appropriate instructor and arrange for private, short-term lessons covering the fundamentals. The instructors have included: (1) a police sergeant who taught self-defense to county officers, (2) a martial arts practitioner who taught an adult continuing education class entitled "Self-Defense Skills for Women," and (3) a martial arts practitioner who taught a course at a local community college. The "classes" for my kids met once a week for about 2 hours, over a period of 6-8 weeks, when they were in middle school.

I strongly encourage you to consider something similar for your child. Joining together with other interested parents and their children can help to keep costs low. The benefits in terms of increased self-confidence are priceless.

6. Effectively Communicate with Your Child on a Daily Basis

There are countless great reasons why it is important to effectively communicate with your child every day about her/his experiences at school. One of the most important is to discuss her/his interaction with the teachers and other school employees. Specifically, it is critical to determine if your requests have been honored (never alone with a school employee and no touching) and if there are any indications that grooming is taking place.

These kinds of conversations are best held with your children while you are interacting in an engaging activity. This could be while baking a cake together, playing a favorite sport/game, or going shopping. The key is to avoid an interrogation-like set of direct questions, but instead interact in a normal and natural manner.

If potential problems surface, you should follow-up with school officials and file formal complaints if warranted.

7. Make Frequent Visits to Your Child's School and Classroom

As frequently as your schedule and workload permit, you should personally visit your child's school and classroom. Such visits clearly communicate your genuine interest in your child's education and welfare to all school employees.

Personal visits allow you to directly observe and evaluate your child's behavior and that of her/his teachers. They enable you to determine if your child is unusually anxious or fearful around a teacher, or unusually affectionate – both potential warning signs.

Your direct observation of the teacher allows you to assess the extent to which grooming is taking place, directed at your child or someone else's. You can also evaluate whether your requests (never alone with a school employee and no touching) are being honored.

Potentially troubling observations should be shared with the principal and teacher. If problems are documented, a formal complaint can be filed requesting disciplinary and corrective action.

There is no substitute for direct personal observation of your child's experiences at school. By "trading off" with other parents, you can insure a steady stream of visitors to her/his classroom, thus also serving as a powerful deterrent to grooming or sexual abuse.

The vigilance of one mother in a recent case in California helped uncover a teacher's sexual abuse. On a periodic basis, she visited her daughter's elementary school to observe educational activities and how her child was performing. On one particular day, while intending to observe her daughter's outdoor gym class, she noticed that neither her daughter nor the male gym teacher were present. Her inquiry as to their whereabouts led to the discovery of the teacher and her daughter in an empty room, playing the "lollipop game". This involved blindfolding the little girl and then having her give him oral sex while he photographed everything. Sadly, this had happened previously on multiple occasions.

8. Chaperones on Field Trips

Field trips away from school, especially those that involve overnight stays, represent a particularly dangerous time for children accompanied by a sexual predator posing as a teacher. Consequently, it is imperative that multiple parent chaperones (of both sexes) participate in all field trips to monitor the behavior of <u>both</u> <u>students</u> and <u>teachers</u>.

Schools should have policies about required parent chaperones, but most don't. Thus, you will need to notify (verbally and in writing) school officials that your child is not authorized to participate in a field trip, unless there are multiple parent chaperones. It can also be very helpful if you are able to occasionally volunteer as a chaperone.

<u>Note</u>: Just as all school employees should be subject to criminal background checks, so should all volunteers who interact with students.

9. Department of Education Advice

Advice offered in the Department of Education (2004) report on educator sexual misconduct includes:

"To increase the possibilities for identification of educator sexual misconduct, educators, parents, and students need to know:

Any employee, including volunteers, might molest.

Educator sexual predators are often well liked and considered excellent teachers.

Special education students or other vulnerable students are often targets of sexual predators.

Adults who have access to students before or after school or in private situations are more likely to sexually abuse students than those who don't (coaches, music teachers, etc.).

Physical signs of sexual abuse include difficulty walking or sitting, torn clothing, stained or bloodied underwear, pain or itching in the genital area, venereal disease, pregnancy, and changes in weight.

Behavioral indicators in students might include age inappropriate sexual behavior, late arrivals to class, changes in personality, and increased time at school with one adult.

Rumors are an important source of information on educator sexual misconduct.

Behaviors of adults who molest include close personal relationships with students, time alone with students, time before or after school with students, time in private spaces with students, flirtatious behavior with students, and off-color remarks in class." (p. 49)

10. Get Other Parents Involved

Pass this information on to other parents who you know, because most are unaware of how serious the sexual abuse problem in schools really is, or how to protect our children.

I firmly believe that knowledge is power. The more parents and children who know about this problem and how to prevent it, the less likely that our daughters and sons are to be sexually abused at school. The more sets of eyes and ears we have monitoring our schools, the less likely educators are to prey on our children.

CONCLUSIONS

As discussed in Chapter 3, sexual predators show a strong preference for children who are passive, shy, lacking in self-confidence, unaware of personal safety issues, and unlikely to complain about being abused. Your personal challenge is to make sure your child does not fit this description. Through education, training, role playing, and parental advice, you can help your daughter or son become more confident, better informed, assertive, and vocal. Together with the other strategies discussed above, this will dramatically reduce the likelihood that your child will be victimized by sexual abuse/harassment at school.

Our shared challenge is to help all children become as victim-proof as possible. Ideally, this effort should be led by our schools. While this is not presently occurring, hopefully we can "motivate" schools to accept and meet this important responsibility.

CHAPTER 9

SURVIVING AND COPING WITH THE TRAUMA OF SEXUAL ABUSE/HARASSMENT

"*There is increasing evidence that, with support from a caring adult and high quality treatment, many children and parents effectively recover and may feel stronger and closer as a family in the aftermath of a {sexually} traumatic experience.*"
Dr. Esther Deblinger
The National Child Traumatic Stress Network, 2009

While there is hope for victims and their families if they seek help, most young people suffer in silence. They don't have the necessary adult support or access to treatment that they desperately need. By failing to address their horrible childhood trauma, many of these individuals carry lifelong wounds that never heal and continue to disrupt their lives.

The primary purpose of this chapter is to clearly communicate the message that victims of K-12 sexual abuse/harassment and their families can fully recover, when provided the necessary support and resources. Success in this critical endeavor involves a three-step process. First, it is essential to understand and acknowledge the seriousness of the trauma experienced by your child and the entire family. Second, it is critical to find a qualified mental health profession to guide and nurture your child's recovery, as well as the family's. Finally, the third step involves a strong commitment by your child and other family members to actively participate in the recovery process. I will describe each of these steps below.

STEP 1 – UNDERSTAND AND ACKNOWLEDGE THE TRAUMA

As discussed in Chapter 1, sexual abuse/harassment often has a devastating impact on K-12 students and their families. Serious psychological, physical/ medical, and behavioral/ school-related problems can quickly develop and prevent a young person from functioning normally, and even last a lifetime.

It is essential that you, as the parent of an injured child, clearly recognize the damaging effects that sexual harassment/abuse can have on your daughter or son. My advice to all parents in this situation is clear and simple – seek professional assistance for your child!

In my opinion, you owe it to your child, yourself, and your family to locate a competent mental health professional to conduct a thorough examination/assessment and implement an effective treatment plan. Early detection and treatment of problems is critical to long-term success.

Perhaps a simple analogy can illustrate why this is so important. If your child were involved in a serious car accident and suffered a deep cut to her abdomen, you would insist on seeing a medical doctor to assess and treat the injury. You would expect an evaluation of possible damage to internal organs, proper cleaning, and suturing of the incision, antibiotics to treat infection, and periodic monitoring to insure full healing. You would never dream of allowing your child's injury to go untreated.

In a similar manner, sexual abuse/harassment can cause grievous psychological injury to your child that can last a lifetime. Often these injuries are not apparent to you or others without the appropriate professional training and experience. Thus, it is imperative that you secure a professional assessment and treatment plan for your child! Qualified help is available. In the next section, I will talk about how to find a good therapist.

STEP 2 — FINDING QUALIFIED PROFESSIONAL ASSISTANCE

Who Qualifies as a Mental Health Professional

Three categories of mental health professionals are qualified, through education, training, and experience, to effectively treat victims of sexual abuse/harassment: (1) psychiatrists, (2) clinical psychologists, and (3) social workers. It is important to note that professionals in all three categories are required to pass licensing exams in the state(s) in which they practice.

Psychiatrists are medical doctors (MD's) who have completed advanced specialized education and training in treating psychological disorders. Clinical psychologists possess one of two closely related doctoral degrees—a Ph.D. or a Psy.D. In both cases, there is comprehensive education and training in dealing with psychological problems. Finally, clinical social workers have a master's degree, or MSW, which involves extensive education and training on methods of diagnosing and treating psychological disorders. Competent individuals in any of these three professions are potential candidates to provide effective assessment and treatment services to your child, yourself, and other members of your family. Suggestions for finding the "right" therapist are discussed in the following section.

Conducting Your Search

Perhaps the best way to locate a good therapist is through referrals from trusted sources. These could include family members, close friends, coworkers, clergy, your family doctor, local hospitals and mental health centers, or a local Children's Advocacy Center (CAC). For a listing of accredited CAC's visit the National Children's Alliance website at http://www.nca-online.org.

If possible, ask your referral sources for two or three recommended therapists in your vicinity. If you hear the same name from multiple sources, this is an individual worthy of consideration.

After securing the names of one or more recommended mental health professionals, it is essential for you to independently assess their credentials and suitability for your child. A critical first step is to contact your state's licensing board to: (1) confirm the therapist's license status and (2) review any misconduct/malpractice complaints and disciplinary records (it is important to note that not all states make this information publically available, although it absolutely should be). The last thing that any parent would want for their traumatized child is a therapist with a prior disciplinary record for abusing clients. Thus, due diligence on your part is clearly called for!

If a therapist candidate "checks out" (properly licensed and a clean disciplinary record), I recommend calling her/his office to confirm that treatment of sexually abused/harassed children and their families is an area of specialty. If so, schedule an initial appointment.

During the first appointment, it is important for you to continue your assessment of her/his suitability by asking questions about: (1) prior experience treating children and their families, (2) recommended psychological evaluations, (3) typical treatment plans and duration, and (4) short-term/long-term success rates. If you are satisfied with the answers provided, and both you and your child are comfortable with the therapist, this person is likely to meet your needs and help your family.

If you are not pleased with the answers to your questions, the therapist seems to resent your questions, or you and your child don't feel comfortable with her/him, exercise your rights as a consumer and continue to search. An inexperienced, incompetent, or unfriendly therapist will only make a bad situation much worse. Don't get discouraged – keep looking until you find the right one!

If your child has been sexually abused, I strongly recommend that you contact the National Child Traumatic Stress Network and consider participating in their outstanding Trauma-Focused Cognitive Behavioral Therapy (TF-CBT) program for children and parents. As a behavioral scientist, I look for treatment programs that have a documented track record of success. The TF-CBT program has consistently generated positive research results and outperformed other treatment options by providing children and their parents with proven strategies to successfully cope and recover from trauma.

Dr. Judith Cohen, one of the three developers of the program, describes its key features at the NCTSN website (www.NCTSN.org, Questions and Answers about Child Sexual Abuse Treatment, p. 2 and 3.):

"Trauma-Focused Cognitive Behavioral Therapy is a structured treatment that takes place over as short a period as twelve weeks. A child and (whenever possible) the child's parent or supportive caregiver participate. The treatment begins with education. The therapist shares information with the child and caregiver about common reactions and symptoms that may result from sexual abuse. This helps children understand that their reactions and feelings are normal and that treatment can help them. It helps parents to accept that the abuse wasn't their fault or the child's fault.

It's common for parents to react to their child's abuse by becoming either too permissive or too protective. The therapist helps them maintain normal routines, household rules, and expectations.

Another step in the treatment, called affect regulation and relaxation, helps the child to identify his or her negative feelings such as anxiety, jumpiness, and sadness that can occur after a trauma. The therapist gives the child techniques to modulate these feelings and to soothe him or herself. This is important so that the child does not begin to withdraw from life to avoid having these feelings.

Another part of the treatment helps children to analyze the connections between their thoughts, feelings, and behaviors. Children who've been sexually abused often feel bad about themselves. They may blame themselves or believe that nothing good will ever happen to them again. We begin by helping children examine their thoughts about everyday events. We then move into exploring their thoughts, beliefs, and feelings about the abuse.

Another part of the therapy is overcoming learned fears. This means unlearning the connection a child has made between the abuser, her negative feelings about it, and trauma reminders, other things and events she's associated with the experience. Desensitization may be necessary when a child continues to have intense reactions to particular things, places, people, or situations that remind him or her of the trauma. To avoid reactions to these trauma reminders, a child may limit his or her experiences. For example, a child may avoid going into the basement of the house where the abuse occurred because she associates the basement with negative feelings about the abuse. Reactions to trauma reminders may also generalize. A child may begin by being afraid to go into the particular basement where the abuse took place, and gradually become afraid of going into any basement, and then into any room that is downstairs or that in any way resembles a basement.

In the case of a child afraid to go into any basement, our treatment would help the child overcome the fear of basements by having the child gradually imagine being in a basement without feeling upset. In some cases, the therapist might actually go into the basement with the child to be sure she can tolerate the experience.

One of the most significant parts of the treatment is the trauma narrative. The clinician helps the child to tell a coherent account of what happened, how it felt, and what it meant. By putting her memories in order, the child no longer feels haunted by them. The therapist helps identify and correct the child's distorted ideas and beliefs about the abuse. For example, an adolescent was in treatment for abuse that occurred when she was five years old and the perpetrator was fifteen. She was still blaming herself for "letting" the abuse occur. By creating the trauma narrative she realized she had been blaming herself for something she hadn't had the power to prevent. By telling the story to her therapist, she corrected her own false understanding. The mother had also felt confused about who was to blame. By sharing this story with her mother in a joint therapy session, the daughter helped her mother to understand what had really happened. The therapy healed not only the young woman but the mother-daughter relationship as well."

If you have unresolved issues as an adult victim of childhood sexual abuse, the TF-CBT program could be very beneficial to you personally. However, your issues would need to be addressed separately, not in the joint sessions with your child.

The research support has been so strong for this approach that the Federal Substance Abuse and Mental Health Services Administration (SAMHSA) has endorsed TF-CBT as a model program and encouraged its use by more mental health practitioners. The National Child Traumatic Stress Network has been training clinicians in use of the TF-CBT program for over twenty years and has trained more than 2,500 individuals.

Finding a TF-CBT trained professional near your home is easy. Just go to the following website (http://www.nctsn.org/resources/get-help-now) and click on <u>Finding Help</u>. You can review the list for your state to find the nearest option. Another approach is to search your phone book for the closest NCTSN site and call for an appointment.

Cost of Therapy

Therapy sessions with a fully qualified and experienced mental health professional are often very expensive, ranging from a low of $75.00 per session to a high of $250.00 or more. However, it is important to emphasize that these costs should be paid for by the school system that allowed the sexual abuse/harassment to occur. Unfortunately, as noted in the 2004 Department of Education (p.45) report on educator misconduct: "Schools rarely provide therapeutic or healing interventions for student victims." If the school system responsible for your child's victimization is unwilling to voluntarily pay for needed therapy, you will need to initiate legal action in civil court to recover these costs. Find a good attorney and sue the school!

In the meantime, most health insurance plans cover all or some portion of the costs for counseling or therapy for your child and the other family members. If your employer has an Employee Assistance Program (EAP), mental health services are typically available for no or low cost.

If you do not have health insurance to pay for counseling, several other potential options are available. First, based upon your financial status, you and your family may qualify for Medicaid, a federal program to provide healthcare to economically disadvantaged individuals. Second, some states offer free healthcare service to children up to the age of 18, depending upon family income. Third, you and your family may qualify for indigent healthcare from publicly-supported hospitals or mental health centers. Finally, you and your family may qualify for a variety of non-profit victim assistance programs. A brief internet search or call to your local United Way could be helpful in identifying appropriate agencies to contact. Fourth, if your child was victimized by criminal sexual abuse, the U.S. Office for Victims of Crime maintains a list of state agencies that have established programs to: (1) assist crime victims in the recovery process, (2) facilitate access to support services, and (3) coordinate available financial assistance.

Don't let cost stop you from getting the professional counseling/ therapy that your child and other family members need to recover from their trauma. Options are available, you just need to be persistent in finding them.

STEP 3 – ACTIVE PARTICIPATION IN THE RECOVERY PROCESS

Success in the process of recovering from sexual harassment/abuse will require active participation from your child, your family, and you. Depending upon the severity and duration, recovery, guided by a competent mental health professional, could require anywhere from a few months to several months or even years in some extreme cases.

Under any circumstances, you need to keep your child, your family, and yourself motivated to attend and participate in scheduled therapy visits, and complete requested therapeutic activities. Your positive, enthusiastic "leadership by example" is essential in communicating to your child and other family members the importance of the therapeutic process. Your genuine, high-energy involvement will help secure and maintain the same level of commitment from your child.

Parental Support

As noted in the opening quote for this chapter, parental support is critical to a child's recovery from sexual harassment/abuse. The National Child Traumatic Stress Network (2010) offers the following guidelines on "trauma-informed" parenting in its educational module entitled "Taking Care of Yourself" (p. 8-16):

"1. Recognize the impact trauma has had on your child.
2. Help your child to feel safe.
3. Help your child to understand and manage overwhelming emotions.
4. Help your child to understand and modify problem behaviors.
5. Respect and support positive, stable, and enduring relationships in the life of your child.
6. Help your child to develop a strength-based understanding of his or her life story.
7. Be an advocate for your child.
8. Promote and support trauma-focused assessment and treatment for your child.
9. Take care of yourself." More on this topic later in the chapter.

Positive Validation and Optimism

Clinical psychologist Stephen Rubin, writing in <u>Teachers That [Who] Sexually Abuse Students</u> (1999, p. 134-135) asserts that parents are especially important in influencing how their child views and interprets a sexual abuse/harassment experience. He recommends communicating with your child, through words and actions, that she is a good person, you love and care for her, you trust her, that what happened was not her fault, that the abusive teacher was the exception, not the rule, and that she will make a full recovery and lead a happy life. In other words, positive, optimistic messages are infectious and can help your child recover more quickly and fully.

Help for Yourself and Other Family Members

As discussed in Chapter 1, when your child is victimized by sexual abuse/harassment, you and everyone else in the family are negatively affected as well. Thus, in addition to supporting and helping your child in the recovery process, it is also important for you to take care of yourself (and other family members) and combat the potential effects of compassion fatigue and Secondary Traumatic Stress (STS). If you allow yourself to become overwhelmed and dysfunctional, you won't be able to effectively provide the love, support, and attention your child (and family) needs to recover.

My colleagues and I have developed a website devoted to managing stress and better understanding its effects on health at http://lifestress.indiana.edu. If you go to the homepage and click on <u>About Coping with Stress</u>, you can access helpful, step-by-step information about how to control and reduce stress levels – both yours and your family's.

Combining information from the above sources, I would highly recommend the following strategies for you and your family members.

1. Be sure to get enough sleep. Most adults need between 7 and 8 hours per night, while children and teens need more.
2. Make sure you and your family eat a well-balanced diet.
3. Try to exercise each day, and if possible, outside during daylight hours. This can help promote sound sleep.

4. Avoid substance abuse, both legal (caffeine, nicotine, and alcohol) and illegal, as this can often worsen the situation.
5. Try to schedule time for breaks to pursue hobbies or other leisure activities.
6. Consider starting (or continuing) a journal/diary to write about what you are experiencing, as a way to organize your thoughts and feelings, and unburden yourself.
7. Try to focus your attention and energy on those events that you can control. If you have no control over something, try not to worry about it.
8. If you have strong spiritual or religious beliefs, they can be very helpful and reassuring during difficult times.
9. Seek social support from individuals you know and trust. Simply sharing what you are experiencing can provide significant relief.
10. Learn and practice stress reduction techniques. At our website, we provide simple instructions for three of the most popular and effective approaches: slow deep breathing, imagery, and progressive relaxation. These techniques, practiced both before and after stressful events, can afford you a tremendous amount of control over the way in which <u>you respond</u> to such situations.
11. If some combination of the above techniques does not work for you or someone in your family, it may be helpful to try counseling or therapy. I recommend this approach be used before seeking medication as a solution due to potential adverse side effects and dependency issues.

As mentioned earlier, if you have personal, unresolved issues as a victim of childhood sexual abuse, the Trauma Focused Cognitive-Behavioral Therapy program could benefit you. Resolution and closure concerning your own victimization would enhance your psychological health and enable you to better support your child.

CONCLUSIONS

Being victimized by sexual abuse/harassment can be a horrifying experience for a young child, with potentially devastating, lifelong consequences. Serious psychological, physical/medical, and behavioral/school-related symptoms can arise that necessitate treatment by qualified mental health professionals.

If your child has been victimized, you owe it to her, other family members, and yourself to seek out a competent therapist to assess the damage and implement an effective treatment plan. Your child needs and deserves a full recovery. Your role, as a parent, is to make sure that happens. Success is achievable, but you need to initiate the process and insure the active participation of everyone involved.

Good luck in returning your child, your family, and yourself to full health.

CHAPTER 10

FIXING SCHOOLS AND WHAT YOU CAN DO TO FIGHT BACK

How evil and heinous is the crime of sexual abuse? Two articles in the Wall Street Journal about recent cases provide some insight about the answer.

"*Experts say incarcerating Mr. Sandusky poses special challenges to prison officials. His age, celebrity and the nature of his crime could make him vulnerable in a population where pedophiles are particularly reviled. 'Pedophiles sit absolutely at the bottom of the prison social structure, and people will go after them,' said David A. Harris, a professor at the University of Pittsburgh School of Law.*" (Monday, June 25, 2012, A3)

"*Authorities say a Texas father won't be charged in the beating death of a man who allegedly molested his 5-year-old daughter. Officials said the Lavaca County grand jury met Tuesday and declined to return an indictment against the father in the death of 47-year-old Jesus Mora Flores. The attack happened on the family's ranch between the farming towns of Shiner and Yoakum. Investigators said the 23-year-old father ran toward his daughter's screams, pulled Mr. Flores off his child and beat him with his hands. Emergency crews found Mr. Flores's pants and underwear pulled down on his lifeless body when they responded to the father's 911 call. The girl was taken to a hospital and examined. Authorities say forensic evidence and witness accounts corroborated the father's story that his daughter was being sexually molested." (Wednesday, June 20, 2012, A6)*

Sexual abuse of a child is an unspeakable crime with a devastating, lifelong impact. We have a moral obligation as a society to protect children from harm and must do whatever is necessary to accomplish this.

Allowing rampant (4.5 million K-12 victims, 2004 Department of Education Report) child sexual abuse by educators to occur in our schools is unconscionable and has to be stopped. As I see it, anyone who sexually abuses children or enables, aids, and abets the sexual abuse of children is my enemy, and should be incarcerated and never allowed to be around children again.

In this chapter, I will discuss a set of aggressive recommendations to stop the problem of child sexual abuse in our schools, and advice about what you can do as a concerned parent. From my perspective, one more victim is one too many.

I will ask everyone to join with me, take appropriate corrective action, and be part of the solution. Unfortunately, I anticipate spirited, even vehement opposition to many of my recommendations. To those who are oppositional and a big part of the problem, I would assertively say that I am unwilling to compromise the safety of school children for any special interest group.

I will discuss my recommendations in the eight major problem categories identified in Chapter 2. These include: (1) School Administrators and Administration, (2) Elected Officials and Applicable Laws, (3) Government Enforcement Agencies, (4) Teachers' Unions, (5) Collegiate Schools of Education, (6) School Accreditation Organizations, (7) State Teacher Certification Agencies, and (8) Teachers.

Before I discuss these eight categories, I want to talk about some recommendations for parents. There are four things that I believe we parents need to do: (1) get informed, (2) get mad, (3) get organized, and (4) get involved.

<u>Get Informed</u> I have had four children and one grandchild in K-12 schools over a 29-year span and I had no idea how many students were victimized by educator sexual misconduct and had never heard of "passing the trash" until this year, in January 2012. One of my primary reasons for writing this book is to make sure other parents become aware of how serious this problem is. We have been kept in the dark for too long! Now we

need to make sure we are as informed as possible about the pandemic of K-12 student sexual abuse/harassment, its causes, and potential solutions. Knowledge is power and we need to acquire knowledge in order to optimally exercise our power.

<u>Get Mad</u> When I first learned about the estimated 4.5 million students who are victimized by educator sexual misconduct, the "passing the trash" deals, the "code of silence" among teachers, and the actual cases of horrible sexual abuse, I was furious.   The thought of one child suffering through the trauma of sexual abuse is hard to bear. The thought of 4.5 million sexual abuse victims is crushing! Many nights, I was so mad that I couldn't sleep. It was hard for me to imagine that this horrendous problem was so enormous and had been going on for so many years.

My anger motivated me to write this book for parents and to search for strategies to stop the abuse. I am confident that parents who read this book will also become mad enough to take action. Many parents have already experienced their children being sexually abused/harassed at school, and many parents were themselves victimized. My heart goes out to all of you. Those of us who have not lived through this hell can certainly empathize with you and feel your pain and anguish.

As parents, we have every reason to be outraged at what has been going on in our schools. My hope is that we can harness and channel this rage into aggressive corrective reforms.

<u>Get Organized</u> There are two important aspects to getting organized. The first involves seeking out other like-minded parents who want to join together and attack the sexual abuse/harassment problem. The more parents who join together, the more we can accomplish and the more power and influence we have, especially at the ballot box when voting for school board members and local/state/national politicians.

The second aspect of getting organized involves systematically considering the resources you have available and determining the best ways to use those resources in attacking the problem. You and your fellow parents may have special talents that allow you to use certain strategies more effectively than others. As you will see in this chapter, there are many things that you could do. The challenge is to find the best fit for your existing resources.

<u>Get Involved</u> This recommendation entails actually implementing the corrective strategies that optimally utilize your existing personal and collective resources. Take action and attack the problem. There is certainly

much that needs to be fixed, so don't delay, but get started as soon as possible. The sexual abusers and those that enable their victimization of children need to know that we won't tolerate it any longer. One more victim is one too many. We need to stop the sexual abuse of our children now!

A few years ago, I participated in a grant-funded program at my son's elementary school called Watch D.O.G.S.—<u>D</u>ads <u>o</u>f <u>G</u>reat <u>S</u>tudents, developed by the National Center for Fathering. The program was designed to get fathers more involved in their children's education.

A criminal background check was conducted on all volunteer dads. If cleared, volunteers were asked to spend a day at the school in their child's classroom(s), observing and helping teachers. It was a very positive experience for everyone involved.

If necessary, a similar program could be developed formally or informally to place parent volunteers in every classroom all day, including after-school activities, to observe and assist teachers. Alternatively, a parent volunteer could be assigned to "shadow" and assist every school employee from their arrival in the morning until their departure from school.

Sexual predators don't abuse their victims in the presence of other adults. A simple program like this would virtually eliminate the probability of educator sexual abuse/harassment of students as well as significantly reduce the incidence of student-on-student abuse/harassment.

Even if enough volunteers were only available for a single day, it would be a Day Without Sexual Abuse/Harassment at School, and send a powerful message to school administrators and employees that parents are dead serious about this issue. Instead of "Occupying Wall Street", parents would "Occupy Schools" in order to stop the sexual abuse/harassment of their children.

I have formulated a Parents' Bill of Rights concerning K-12 student sexual abuse/harassment, in Figure 10-1 below. It summarizes 15 essential rights that I feel every parent is entitled to and should already have. Sadly, schools have never provided these fundamental rights to parents and probably never will, on a voluntary basis. If you agree with me about these rights, ask your school board or superintendent about them. We will likely need new laws to force schools to guarantee these rights for parents. Or, perhaps a concerned, energized school board would be bold enough to do this on their own. Good luck with yours.

FIGURE 10-1

Parents of K-12 Students Bill of Rights

Concerning Sexual Abuse/Harassment

All <u>parents</u> of K-12 students should be guaranteed the following rights concerning sexual abuse/harassment:

1. The <u>right</u> to receive and review, prior to the enrollment of their daughter/son in a school system, published summary statistics on the incidence of documented sexual abuse/harassment cases at the institution.

2. The <u>right</u> to know that no employee in the school system has a prior criminal or disciplinary record for sexual abuse/harassment.

3. The <u>right</u> to know that anyone hired by the school for full-time/part-time jobs or volunteer positions has successfully passed a fingerprint-based national criminal check and thorough assessment of previous employers, to include prior disciplinary issues.

4. The <u>right</u> to know that their daughter/son will receive age-appropriate <u>mandatory</u> annual training on sexual abuse/harassment, to include:
    1. a clear statement of student rights and responsibilities,
    2. specific guidelines concerning appropriate and inappropriate employee behaviors,
    3. simple instructions concerning how and where to file a complaint, and
    4. a full explanation of options to initiate civil and/or criminal charges, along with applicable filing deadlines.

5. The <u>right</u> to know that all school employees and volunteers have successfully completed a <u>mandatory</u> annual training program on sexual abuse/harassment, to include:

1. specific responsibilities, including reporting,
2. clear guidelines concerning appropriate and inappropriate behaviors, and
3. the serious disciplinary consequences for those who violate student rights or fail to report violations.

6. The right to available training for parents on school-based sexual abuse/harassment.

7. The right to have a truly student-friendly complaint process that encourages victims to come forward.

8. The <u>right</u> to know that <u>all complaints</u> (both formal or informal) concerning <u>alleged</u> sexual abuse/harassment conduct will be <u>competently</u>, <u>confidentially</u>, and <u>thoroughly</u> investigated in a timely manner by qualified professionals, to include contacting <u>former students</u> who may have been victimized, or who may have information relevant to the complaint.

9. The <u>right</u> to know that school employees <u>charged</u> with sexual abuse/harassment will be immediately removed from any positions involving student contact, pending the results of a full investigation.

10. The <u>right</u> to know that students found guilty of sexual abuse/harassment will be appropriately disciplined (including suspension or expulsion, depending upon offense severity and frequency).

11. The <u>right</u> to know that school employees found guilty of sexual abuse/harassment will be appropriately disciplined (including termination, depending upon offense frequency and severity).

12. The <u>right</u> to know that school employees who are aware of suspected sexual abuse/harassment, but fail to report it, will be disciplined, up to and including termination.

13. The <u>right</u> to know that their daughter/son (and the entire family if necessary) will receive counseling/therapy, if victimized by sexual abuse/harassment at school, paid for by the institution.

14. The <u>right</u> to know that their daughter/son will be protected from any attempted retaliation for filing a complaint, initiated by the alleged abuser/harasser or his supporters.

15. The <u>right</u> to know that their daughter/son will be protected after filing a complaint, from any continuing sexual abuse/harassment, initiated by the alleged abuser/harasser and/or his supporters.

I have also prepared two sample letters that you might consider sending to your superintendent and/or school board. The first letter (Figure 10-2) asks for written responses to four critical questions that all parents should want answers to. The second letter (Figure 10-3) is much more aggressive. It strongly communicates that sexual abuse/harassment of your child or any child should not occur and promises swift legal action, holding the superintendent and school board fully responsible, if any student is victimized. Modify either of the letters to suit your situation and use them if you feel they will be helpful.

FIGURE 10-2

Letter #1

School Superintendents and School Board Presidents

My name is _____ and my child(ren) attends the _____ school system. As a parent, I am very concerned about the sexual abuse/harassment of students by school teachers and employees. I want to insure that this does not happen to my child(ren) or anyone's children within our school district.

I would like to ask you four questions and request that you provide written answers to each one.

1. Does the school system currently employ anyone (full or part-time) who has a prior record for sexual abuse, sexual harassment, or sexual misconduct? If "yes", why have you placed my child and other children at risk by this sexual predator?
2. Does the school system currently employ anyone (full or part-time) against whom formal and/or informal complaints have been lodged, alleging sexual abuse, sexual harassment, or sexual misconduct and no action has been taken by the administration? If "yes", the individual(s) involved needs to be immediately suspended (with full pay) until a comprehensive, professional investigation has been conducted.
3. Does the school system conduct the following pre-employment procedures before hiring any new employee: (1) a fingerprint-based national criminal background check and (2) a complete assessment of all previous employment, to include disciplinary action/charges/investigation/pending investigation for sexual abuse, sexual harassment, or sexual misconduct? If "no", why are these steps to protect the welfare of our students not taken?
4. Does the school system require all volunteers and substitute teachers to have a fingerprint-based national criminal background check? If "no", why not?

I look forward to receiving your responses and the opportunity to work with you to protect the safety of our students.

If any questions arise, please contact me at: _____.

Sincerely,

FIGURE 10-3

Letter #2

School Superintendents and School Board Presidents

My name is _____ and my child(ren) attends the _____ school system. As a parent, I am very concerned about the sexual abuse and sexual harassment of students by school teachers and employees. I want to insure that this does not happen to my child(ren) or anyone's children within our school district.

I am familiar with the U.S. Department of Education Report, entitled "Educator Sexual Misconduct: A Synthesis of Existing Literature" (2004) and its disturbing findings:

1. an estimated 4.5 million children are victimized by educator sexual abuse in grades K-12,
2. teachers rarely report other teachers who illegally sexually abuse children,
3. school administrators rarely report teachers who illegally sexually abuse children to the police, and,
4. school administrators often negotiate with teachers who sexually abuse children to resign in exchange for a positive letter of reference and no reporting to police.

None of this illegal and reprehensible conduct should be occurring in our school district! If it does and one child is victimized (mine or anyone else's), I will hold you directly and personally responsible, and will take the following legal actions and/or encourage other parents to do likewise.

1. I will request that full criminal charges be filed against the child sexual abuser.
2. I will aggressively seek criminal charges for aiding and abetting a child abuser, being an accessory to child sexual abuse, conspiracy to commit child sexual abuse, criminal negligence in hiring, criminal negligence in supervision, and/or criminal negligence in retention

against <u>you</u>, and any other administrators, teachers, or union officials who knew or should have known about the sexual abuse and did nothing.
3. I will file a complaint against the school district on behalf of my child with the Office for Civil Rights in the U.S. Department of Education for a violation of Title IX of the 1972 Education Amendments, and ask for a full investigation and corrective action.
4. I will file a complaint against the school district on behalf of my child with the U.S. Department of Justice for a civil rights violation, and ask for a full investigation and corrective action.
5. I will file legal action in federal court against the school district on behalf of my child for a violation of Title IX of the 1972 Education Amendments.
6. I will file civil legal action in federal court against the perpetrator, <u>you personally</u>, and any other administrators, union official, and/or teachers who knew about the sexual abuse under the provisions of the Equal Protection Clause of the 14th Amendment to the Constitution, 42 U.S.C. §1983, and 18 U.S.C. §241.
7. I will file civil legal action in state court against the perpetrator, <u>you personally</u>, and any other administrators who knew about the sexual abuse and did nothing for all of the following that apply: (a) assault, (b) battery, (c) false imprisonment, (d) invasion of privacy, (e) professional malpractice, (f) intentional infliction of emotional distress, (g) breach of contract, (h) negligent hiring, (i) negligent supervision, and (j) negligent retention.

I know what my legal rights are and I will fully exercise them if my child or any child in our school district is victimized by educator sexual abuse. I hope for everyone's sake that the school district does not have any serial child sexual abusers on-staff and in contact with our students, and that you have exercised due diligence in thoroughly assessing the background and prior employment of anyone hired by the school district.

If so, congratulations on doing your job and protecting our students from sexual abusers. If not, you need to take immediate and aggressive corrective action or face the consequences.

My concerns also extend to sexual abuse initiated by students. Again, I expect that you have effective programs in place to: (1) train students about their rights and responsibilities, (2) monitor student behavior, (3) initiate prompt corrective action if student misconduct occurs, and (4) remove students who pose a threat to others from our school system.

If questions arise, or you would like to discuss any of these issues, please contact me at: _____.

Sincerely,

Let's talk now about specific recommendations in the eight categories listed above.

1. School Administrators and Administration

School Administrators

In this group, I include superintendents and school board members. I have a lot to say to these individuals and several recommendations.

First, if you have negotiated or approved "passing the trash" deals in the past, those wrongs need to be corrected immediately. However belatedly, report the abuser to police. Identify past victims in your school system, apologize, and offer free access to professional counseling services. Contact the school(s) the abuser went to, based upon your favorable recommendation, tell the truth, apologize, and offer to assist victims. Turn yourself in to the police. Serve your sentence for failure to notify police. Look for work in another field that does not involve children.

If school administrators who have negotiated or approved "passing the trash" deals in the past don't come forward now, they face prosecution to the fullest extent to the law when their illegal conduct is discovered.

Second, I have formulated a sample pledge for superintendents and school board members concerning sexual abuse/harassment issues in school. I recommend using a document like this in hiring/retaining superintendents and electing/retaining school board members.

FIGURE 10-4

Sample Pledge for Superintendents and School Board Members

As a Superintendent/School Board Member, I Pledge To:

1. Personally report any suspected case of child sexual abuse to law enforcement authorities.
2. Never allow a "passing the trash" deal to be negotiated with child sexual abusers.
3. Support and enforce a zero-tolerance policy on sexual abuse/harassment of students, with discipline proportional to the offense committed by violators.
4. Insure that any employee who fails to report suspected child sexual abuse to law enforcement authorities <u>and</u> school administrators is disciplined.
5. Insure that all new hires complete thorough national criminal background checks and rigorous reference checking with prior employers.
6. Insure that sexual abuse/harassment training is provided annually to all school employees, all students, and interested parents.
7. Support and enforce school policies on employees never being alone with students and appropriate touching of students by employees, with discipline for violators.
8. Conduct and publish results of an annual sexual abuse/harassment survey of students.
9. Publish annual incidence rates of student sexual abuse/harassment.
10. Assemble and publish an annual summary of sexual abuse/harassment cases and outcomes (without individual names).

In my opinion, if a prospective or current superintendent cannot commit to protecting the safety and welfare of children, I would not recommend hiring or retaining such and individual. The same applies to school board members.

You or the PTO/PTA could propose the use of such a pledge with the superintendent and school board members in your district. If they don't support any of the items in the pledge, I would ask for a public explanation.

School Administration

My recommendations concerning school administration will be organized in the same manner as the school rating scale contained in Appendix B. Thus, I will offer suggestions pertinent to:

1. Formal Institutional Policies,
2. Sexual Abuse/Harassment Training,
3. Student Support Services,
4. Complaint Processing and Investigations, and
5. Discipline, Public Reporting and Information Dissemination.

<u>Formal School Policies</u> I have five specific recommendations concerning formal school policies. As a parent, if these recommendations are applicable to your school, I suggest that you make an appropriate request to your superintendent or school board.

1. It is essential that schools have a carefully crafted, zero-tolerance policy on sexual abuse/harassment that is widely distributed to students, employees, and parents. The policy should contain examples of prohibited conduct, clear instructions on complaint filing, mandatory reporting requirements for all employees, disciplinary consequences for violators, and retaliation protection for complaints.
2. Every school should have a strongly worded policy prohibiting employees from being alone with students under any circumstances.
3. Schools should have research-based, psychologically sound policies on appropriate and inappropriate teacher touching of students. Most professionals agree that after elementary school, teacher touching should be largely eliminated.
4. Schools should have a strict policy requiring at least one male and female parent chaperones be present on all field trips.

5. I have witnessed on several occasions the negative effects of a poorly written and/or improperly enforced student dress code on the overall climate within a school, primarily in high school. Allowing students to wear provocative or revealing clothing creates a sexually-charged environment, conducive to sexual abuse/harassment. Thus, I highly recommend that every school system have a comprehensive dress code that explicitly prohibits inappropriate clothing and is strictly enforced. As a parent, visit your high school in the fall or late spring to get a first-hand impression of dress code enforcement, and initiate a complaint with the principal, superintendent, or school board if corrective action is needed.

<u>Hiring Recommendations</u> The overwhelming majority of a school's problems with educator sexual abuse/harassment of children could be prevented with comprehensive screening in the hiring process. With this in mind, I offer the following specific recommendations and encourage you to submit them to your school board or superintendent.

1. All applicants for school employment should be required to undergo a fingerprint-based national criminal background check and pay for it themselves. This requirement can cause individuals with criminal records to withdraw from the application process. Obviously, anyone with a documented prior criminal record would be excluded from further consideration.
2. Application forms for all school positions should clearly state that information provided will be subject to verification and that providing false or incomplete information will result in exclusion from the application process or immediate termination if already hired.
3. Application forms for all school positions should contain the following question, designed explicitly to stop "passing the trash":

"Have you ever been disciplined for misconduct involving students by a previous employer, chosen to resign rather than face discipline for misconduct involving students, resigned while under investigation for misconduct involving students, or resigned after complaints were filed against you for misconduct involving students? If yes, please explain fully." My experience with this type of question in other work settings is that many males voluntarily withdraw from the application process rather than respond.

4. Applicants for school positions should personally sign a "waiver of liability" letter to all former employers, requesting a complete reference and holding them legally harmless for the content. Once again, my experience with this practice in other employment settings is that many individuals withdraw from the application process.
5. The field of industrial/organizational psychology has made great strides over the last 20 years in developing psychological tests to substantially improve accuracy in the hiring process. I firmly believe that a well-formulated, research-based personality test could be a valuable addition to the screening process for school employees by identifying individuals with a high propensity for sexually abusing/harassing children.

Let me give you an example of how psychological testing was successfully used in a similarly challenging work environment. Nearly 30 years ago, a TV station in a large Midwestern city conducted an investigation of police brutality to determine who was responsible, what it cost, and how it could be prevented.

As is the case with educator sexual abuse/harassment, the investigation revealed that a tiny percentage of all police officers were responsible for most of the brutality cases. With a strong union backing them, it was very difficult for the city to terminate the offenders. Rather, they were often transferred to other precincts ("passing the trash") and the brutality reoccurred, over and over again.

The physical injuries sustained by savagely beaten victims were horrific. The lawsuits brought in these cases were costing the city millions of dollars annually.

Surprisingly, and unlike other major cities at the time, this municipal police department did not do any psychological screening of applicants. Thus, one of the recommendations made as a result of the investigation was that the city begin using psychological tests to identify those applicants with a high propensity to abuse their authority and brutalize citizens.

A test with a record of success in other large cities was identified. Its use over the next five years did result in significantly fewer charges of police brutality against the newly hired officers and substantially lower legal and settlement expenses.

Although there is no psychological test presently designed for use in screening school applicants, there are several tests that are utilized in our legal system to make decisions about convicted sex offenders; for example, what risk do they pose to others if paroled or released from prison. I have written to the publishers of these instruments and inquired about their interest in developing and validating such an assessment tool. To date, I have not yet found one interested in doing this.

In my opinion, psychological testing would be an invaluable addition to current screening procedures by helping to identify those individuals most likely to sexually abuse children. The presence of such a tool in the hiring process would also act to discourage child abusers from applying. Given the high potential of this approach to dramatically reduce the incidence of child sexual abuse/harassment (and the horrible harm that is done) and significantly lower the associated financial costs to schools, I will continue the search for an interested test publisher.

Perhaps the American Psychological Association or its Division 14, the Society for Industrial and Organizational Psychology, could be approached about overseeing the development of such a tool as a public service project of national importance.

6. As part of the hiring process for school employees, I recommend a longer probationary period, during which time closer supervision and performance monitoring should occur to screen for potential signs of abuse/harassment. The enhanced monitoring must include collecting feedback from students, parents, and other employees.
7. Given the conclusive research finding that the overwhelming majority of child sexual abusers are male, schools should consider enhanced screening procedures for male applicants. I fully understand the value and need for men as teachers and role models in the educational process. However, in view of the substantial additional risk of child sexual abuse associated with males, additional hiring requirements would be prudent. This could perhaps take the form of more thorough psychological screening.

Given that male coaches have the highest rates of sexual abuse for any teachers, I would either: (1) ban male coaches entirely from female sports teams or (2) assign an adult female <u>co-coach</u> in every instance, to be present at all team activities.

Once hired, males should be monitored more closely by school administrators to detect early signs of student grooming or abuse and initiate corrective action immediately. This monitoring should include direct observation of interaction with students and the solicitation of feedback from students, parents, and colleagues.

I understand that these recommendations will arouse strong condemnation from many men. Remember however, my goal is to stop the sexual abuse/harassment of K-12 students. Men are the perpetrators of virtually all of this abuse. Thus, additional protective measures for children are demanded. If some men or male coaches don't like this, I'm sorry, the safety and welfare of children come first!

My fundamental question about "passing the trash" deals is why do school districts hire "trash" in the first place? More rigorous selection screening can help schools deny employment to "trash", thus preventing problems before they occur.

<u>Training</u> Efforts to prevent sexual abuse/harassment in K-12 must include mandatory annual training for all stakeholder groups, focused solely on the school environment, showing school teachers, employees, volunteers, and students as potential abusers/harassers. These stakeholder groups include: (1) all school employees, (2) substitute teachers, (3) volunteers, (4) administrators and school board members, and (5) parents.

Clearly, training for students must be age-appropriate, with understandable content and examples. Training for parents could be a mandatory part of the school registration process, with a child's parent(s) required to view a video about K-12 sexual abuse/harassment and invited to attend a longer session on the subject, if interested.

At a bare minimum, the following topics should be addressed in an interactive manner during the training:

1. the school's zero-tolerance policy on sexual abuse/harassment,
2. the definition of sexual abuse/harassment, along with relevant examples in the school environment,
3. the school's policy on employees touching students,

4. the school's policy on employees not being alone with students,
5. persons who could abuse/harass, including teachers, administrators, other school employees, and students,
6. complaint filing options – how, with whom, and contact information,
7. the grooming process,
8. how to protect oneself from sexual abuse/harassment,
9. proper and improper roles/boundaries for employees and students,
10. protection from retaliation for complaint filers,
11. efforts to keep complaint information confidential,
12. all complaints are investigated in a timely manner,
13. disciplinary outcomes commensurate with the severity of the offense, up to termination for employees and expulsion for students,
14. potential criminal violations are referred to the police,
15. the responsibility of all employees to report suspected child sexual abuse to the police and school administration,
16. the disciplinary consequences for employees who fail to report suspected child sexual abuse, and
17. a summary of the most recent annual:
    a) student sexual abuse/harassment survey,
    b) sexual abuse/harassment incidence statistics, and
    c) sexual abuse/harassment case outcomes summary.

I would also like to see basic self-defense training offered annually to all K-12 children. This would help to build self-confidence and provide the skills necessary to respond to an attempted sexual attack.

<u>Student Support Services</u> Schools have done a disgraceful job in providing counseling and support services to victims of sexual abuse/harassment. If children are victimized at school by school employees or poorly monitored students, the district has a responsibility to provide immediate assistance.

If a child falls down at school and breaks a leg, emergency medical care is quickly provided. It would be unthinkable for the school to allow the child to continue suffering, provide no treatment, and not inform parents.

The psychological (and perhaps physical) wounds of sexual abuse/harassment are equally painful and traumatic. Immediate attention is thus also needed to stop the damage and begin the healing process. Consequently, counseling and other support services need to be easily and immediately accessible to children, with referrals to local mental health providers, as appropriate.

<u>Complaint Filing and Investigations</u> It is essential that schools create complaint filing systems that encourage victims to come forward. This should entail: (1) multiple complaint filing options, including any teacher or administrator and an anonymous option, (2) the promise that all complaints will be investigated, (3) a pledge that confidentiality will be maintained to the maximum extent possible, (4) an assurance that the complainant will be protected from retaliation, and (5) the provision of immediate counseling services to complainants, as needed.

In terms of complaint investigations, my recommendations include:

(1) the investigator should be a trained professional, hired from outside the school district, in order to insure that a thorough, unbiased investigation is conducted,
(2) the investigation should be conducted in a timely manner and concluded within 7-10 days of the complaint, and
(3) any evidence uncovered in the investigation suggesting criminal violations should be immediately provided to law enforcement authorities.

<u>Discipline</u> Zero-tolerance for sexual abuse/harassment means that every policy violation results in disciplinary action, with the severity of the discipline commensurate with the seriousness of the offense. Flagrant or repeated violations should result in termination for employees and expulsion for students.

Failure to report suspected child sexual abuse/harassment and violations of the school's employee touching and alone with students policies must also result in progressive disciplinary actions. For repeated violations of these policies, an employee could be suspended or referred for a mandatory "fitness for duty" evaluation by a mental health professional and not allowed back in the workplace until "cleared" as not posing a threat to student safety and welfare.

It is not enough to simply include discipline in a school policy and talk about it in training programs; administrators must discipline any policy violators. As Dr. Louise Fitzgerald and her team of researchers have repeatedly demonstrated, serious disciplinary consequences for violators consistently result in lower incidence rates of sexual abuse/harassment. Disciplinary action, especially in egregious cases when termination or expulsion are clearly warranted, sends a powerful message to school employees and students that the administration has zero-tolerance for sexual abuse/harassment and will impose stiff discipline, including termination or expulsion, for any offenders. Every school needs to create such an environment, in which everyone knows that sexual abuse/harassment will not be tolerated!

<u>Public Reporting and Information Dissemination</u> The general public, students, parents, and tax payers all have a right to know about the pandemic of K-12 student sexual abuse/harassment in our schools. We need to demand this information from superintendents and school boards. If they are not willing to provide this information they should be replaced! Hopefully, executive orders will be signed or federal and/or state laws will be passed in the near future requiring schools to provide complete information to the public. This should include:

(1) annual incidence rates of student sexual abuse/harassment,
(2) annual summaries of sexual abuse/harassment complaints and outcomes, without names, and
(3) annual results of student sexual abuse/harassment surveys.

Only by having this data available will we know how bad the problem is in a particular school system and whether progress is made over time in addressing it. Full disclosure is critical to stopping the disgraceful sexual abuse/harassment of our K-12 students.

Tenure

As I argued in Chapter 2, tenure is a major reason why schools are not able to effectively discipline and terminate teachers who sexually abuse/harass students, leading to "pass the trash" deals. Consequently, states need to substantially modify their tenure statutes to allow schools to fire sexual predators in a timely, cost-effective manner. If such modifications are not made, public opinion could turn decidedly negative toward teacher tenure, potentially resulting in legislative attempts to ban it. Teachers' unions can be expected to vigorously oppose any efforts to revise tenure laws. This is very unfortunate, as revisions are desperately needed to better protect children. Supporting the rights of sexual predators masquerading as teachers, over those of innocent children, is just plain wrong and will only serve to reinforce the continuing national decline in support for unions.

Financial Mismanagement

In Chapter 2, I talked about the huge costs associated with school mismanagement of the sexual abuse/harassment problem—costs that are hidden from the public. I recommend that school districts and/or states require that the costs associated with sexual abuse/harassment of students be made publically available on an annual basis and posted at the school's website. Let's shine a spotlight on this hidden problem and force schools to be accountable.

Until school districts and states are required to publish this information, I recommend that you individually request an accounting of these costs from your school system (and state) for the last 5 years, along with an explanation of why this information was never made available previously. Your request should include the following specific items:

1. damage awards and financial settlements,
2. annual premiums for liability insurance covering sexual abuse/harassment,
3. legal fees for outside attorneys and/or the dollar value of the time spent by school attorneys,
4. the dollar value of the time spent on these cases by school administrators and employees,
5. the costs of supplies and equipment used, and
6. the cost of any expert witnesses required.

If you are successful in obtaining this information, prepared to be shocked and outraged. With tight school budgets everywhere in the country, there is no excuse for spending scarce resources due to school management's inability to effectively prevent and correct the sexual abuse/harassment of students. There are strategies to stop this problem and administrators need to be held strictly accountable for doing so, while properly managing the school budget to maximize the educational experience of students.

Sue Former Teachers and/or Administrators for Damages Paid by School Districts

The Equal Employment Opportunity Commission (EEOC) represented 80 females employed at Astra USA, in a 1998 case alleging widespread sexual harassment against the firm and its CEO, Lars Bildman. The company agreed to settle the case for 10 million dollars, fired the CEO, and immediately initiated a civil lawsuit against him for $15 million to recover the costs of the settlement, its legal fees, and the adverse publicity.

In 1996, William and Mary College and Virginia Commonwealth University both filed lawsuits against faculty members who had been fired for sexually harassing students. The harassment had resulted in substantial damage awards to the victims. Schools argued that the offending professors were personally responsible for the entire damages awarded.

I use these examples in sexual harassment prevention training for managers and professors to clearly communicate the substantial personal financial risks associated with sexual misconduct. Similar civil lawsuits could function as a powerful deterrent to teachers contemplating sexual misconduct and administrators planning "passing the trash" deals.

Thus, I highly recommend that schools communicate to all of their administrators and employees that civil lawsuits will be initiated to recover damages paid as a result of employee or administration sexual abuse/harassment. We then need schools to follow-up on this promise and actually file such lawsuits. Taxpayers should demand such a strategy as a routine business practice to recover public funds spent in damage awards. Therefore, you could recommend and insist that this approach be utilized within your school district.

Liability Insurance Firms

Schools purchase liability insurance to protect themselves from the costs associated with cases involving the sexual abuse/harassment of students. As with any other type of insurance, schools pay an annual premium, based upon the predicted risk they pose.

Insurance companies could drive the reforms needed to better protect students by offering substantially lower premiums to those schools that effectively implemented necessary preventive and corrective actions. In fact, insurance firms could offer programs to schools to help them identify major risks and put programs in place to minimize them. The school rating scale in Appendix B could be used to assess the likelihood of risk and guide corrective actions. Schools could be rewarded for earning higher scores with lower premiums.

You could challenge your superintendent or school board to approach their insurance carrier about the possibility of substantially lowering premiums if certain preventive steps are taken. If the insurance firm does not respond favorably, I would rebid the contract and seek other firms that would work with the school system to lower premiums.

2. Elected Officials and Laws

The U.S. president and state governors have broad powers to regulate organizations that receive government funding. Our president or any state governor could issue an "executive order", covering all schools that receive federal or state funding, that directs these institutes to implement specific reform policies and procedures designed to better protect children, as a condition for receiving government funds.

For example, President Johnson issued Executive Order 11246 in 1965 that directed organizations receiving federal contracts valued at $10,000 or more to implement specific procedures to prevent workplace discrimination. In a similar manner, President Obama, or any state governor, could issue an executive order directing that schools: (1) ban the practice of "passing the trash", (2) require national fingerprint-based criminal background checks in the hiring process, (3) provide annual sexual abuse/harassment training to all employees, students, and parents, (4) provide accurate references for previous employees, (5) allow complaints to be filed with any teacher or administrator, (6) implement and enforce policies on teachers being alone with students and appropriate touching of students by teachers, and (7) publish annual sexual abuse/harassment statistics.

An executive order is certainly more expedient than trying to get supportive laws passed through contentious legislatures. All that is needed is a supportive, energized president or governor, unafraid of political fallout and opposition from teachers' unions.

Congress and/or state legislatures could pass laws to improve the protection of children in our schools. Topics for new legislation could include those discussed above. In addition, new laws are needed at the national (or state) level to:

(1) lower the legal requirements necessary to establish school liability in sexual abuse/harassment cases, especially "deliberate indifference" and the need to prove that the abuse/harassment was "severe, pervasive, and objectively offensive",
(2) hold schools legally responsible for all of the actions taken by teachers and other professionals,
(3) increase criminal penalties for educators who fail to report suspected child sexual abuse,

"Florida Passes Stringent Reporting Law for Suspected Child Sex Abuse. Florida now boasts the strictest mandatory reporting law for suspected child sex abuse, under a measure signed by Gov. Rick Scott on April 27. The Protection of Vulnerable Persons Act, which takes effect Oct 1, tightens requirements for reporting known or suspected abuse of a child and raises the criminal penalties for individuals who fail to report such abuse from a misdemeanor to a third-degree felony. The law applies to anyone and everyone who suspects or knows of child abuse and 'willfully and knowingly' fails to report it. For more information, go to http://www.myfloridahouse.gov, click on 'Find a Bill' and enter 1355."

(Thompson's Educator's Guide to Controlling Sexual Harassment, June 2012)

More states need to follow Florida's lead in increasing the criminal penalties for failure to report child sexual abuse by educators. In addition to tougher laws, we need prosecutors who are willing to file charges against those who fail to meet this critical legal responsibility.

The Florida example is one of an increasing number of encouraging signs that our society has had enough with school predators and won't take anymore. In my opinion, parents need to be the driving force and lead national, state, and local initiatives,

(4) substantially increase the enforcement authority of the U.S. Office for Civil Rights (OCR), so as to be equivalent to that of the Equal Employment Opportunity Commission (EEOC), especially the power to sue schools on behalf of student victims.

(5) significantly increase the budget of the OCR to allow for both more extensive preventive efforts and increased legal action against offending schools, and

(6) reduce the burden on children to testify repeatedly about the alleged abuse, which only serves to revictimize them and prolong their recovery.

Given the continuing gridlock in Congress, successful legislative action is more likely at the state level. You can start this process by contacting and lobbying with your state legislators.

Below are two recent encouraging examples of bills introduced (one in the U.S. House of Representatives and one in New York) by concerned legislators, to address the sexual abuse/harassment pandemic in our schools. I hope these bills pass and I hope others like them are introduced and passed as well.

Both of these examples are from Thompson's <u>Educator's Guide to Controlling Sexual Harassment,</u> July 2012, p. 8:

> "*House Bill Would Bar Employer Relocation of Sex Offenders. A bill introduced late last year in the U.S. House of Representatives would amend the federal criminal code to bar employers from encouraging employees who engage in sexual conduct with underage persons to relocate to another state. The Jeremy Bell Act of 2011 also would require both private and public schools and education agencies to adopt policies that ensure that all of their employees undergo a fingerprint-based check of the national crime information databases and of state criminal history databases. The bill would condition receipt of Elementary and Secondary Education Act funds on enforcement of a state law that ensures all of the following:*
>
> - *That schools report to law enforcement officials any incidents of sexual conduct involving a minor and a school employee;*
> - *That schools that fail to report such incidents are penalized;*

- *That states report to an interstate clearinghouse the identity of school employees investigated for sexual conduct involving a minor and whose employment was terminated as a result; and*
- *That such information is only made available to schools and educational agencies, and not the general public.*

The bill was introduced by Rep. Michael Fitzpatrick (R-Pa.) and referred to the House Subcommittee on Early Childhood, Elementary and Secondary Education March 29. It currently has seven cosponsors. For more information, go to http://thomas.loc.gov and search for 'Jeremy Bell Act.'"

"N.Y. Bill Would Make it Easier to Fire Teachers Accused of Sexual Misconduct. In New York, there is a push for state legislation to make it easier to dismiss teachers who engage in sexual misconduct with students. Sponsored by State Sen. Stephen Saland and supported by New York City Mayor Michael Bloomberg, the bill would give school districts the power to decide whether a teacher accused of sexual misconduct should be fired. Currently, outside hearing officers have this authority, and school districts must abide by the hearing officer's decision.

The reform would amend New York State Education Law 3020 – so that school districts – and in New York City, the Schools' Chancellor – have the final say on what action to take. In a press release, Bloomberg said the Department of Education has been prevented from terminating teachers in cases where the City's own independent investigator found instances of inappropriate sexual conduct.

'If a school employee is found to have engaged in sexual behavior or made sexual comments towards students, the Chancellor should have the final say on what action to take, and the legislation we are proposing would provide that authority,' said Mayor Bloomberg. 'Every child deserves a safe learning environment and every parent has the right to know that his or her child is safe while at school,' he said."

3. Government Enforcement Agencies

If the Office for Civil Rights (OCR) is to be realistically charged with protecting K-12 children from sexual abuse/harassment, major changes are needed. I recommend that the OCR prepare a report for Congress summarizing the pandemic nature of the problem, the limits of its capabilities to address the problem, and specifically what is required to substantially enhance its presence and effectiveness in K-12 schools. For example, the statistic for FY 2008, indicating that no complaints of sexual abuse/harassment were received from K-12 students, strongly suggests that the OCR is a non-entity in this critical domain.

Clearly, the enforcement authority of the OCR must be significantly enhanced (the power to sue schools on behalf of students) if it is to successfully perform its mission. In addition, large increases in staff and budget are necessary to "extend the reach" of the OCR and firmly establish its role in protecting children.

For prosecutors, I would strongly recommend that they give K-12 sexual abuse/harassment cases their highest priority. We need a concerted national effort to stop sexual predators from harming our children and hold enabling non-reporters criminally accountable as well.

4. Teachers' Unions

My recommendation to teachers' unions is quite simple: Stop protecting teacher sexual predators and allowing them to stay in the classroom, where they continue to abuse innocent students. Until this happens, unions will find themselves in an indefensible, very unpopular position.

While unions have historically served critically important roles in our country's development, the number of union members and support for unions have fallen dramatically in recent years. If unions choose to continue fighting to keep sexual predators in teaching positions, national support will fall to new lows.

Failing to report suspected child sexual abuse to police and negotiating "passing the trash deals" are illegal and immoral. Union officials, and anyone else, who participates in these unlawful activities should be incarcerated.

I advise union leaders to think long and hard about these issues and abandon illegal indefensible practices. Unions could play a significant positive role in formulating solutions to the pandemic of K-12 student sexual abuse/harassment, or they could choose to obstruct needed reforms and remain a big part of the problem.

I believe I speak for most parents when I say, we will not compromise on student safety and welfare. This has to come first. Anything that jeopardizes or threatens child safety and welfare must be aggressively fought. I personally look forward to collaborating with union leaders to address this national problem, while at all times vigorously protecting student safety and welfare.

For those union leaders who have participated in negotiating "passing the trash" deals and failed to notify police, I have the following specific recommendation. Those past wrongs need to be corrected immediately. Contact police and report the suspected abuse now! Assist authorities in identifying past student victims, so that they can get professional counseling and support services. Apologize to them for turning your back on their suffering. Turn yourself in to the police and serve your sentence. Vow never to abandon children and fail to report abuse again. If you don't come forward, when your illegal conduct is discovered, you face prosecution to the fullest extent of the law.

5. Collegiate Schools of Education

This is the first door through which sexual predators must pass in their quest to have easy access to young students. Teachers who fail to report sexual abuse/harassment and administrators who both fail to report and negotiate "passing the trash" deals also pass through the collegiate school of education door. Thus, I have several recommendations about how to improve this process.

I would suggest that college officials and faculty take these recommendations seriously. One way to further motivate reform efforts is to routinely report the college from which convicted child sexual abusers and colluding/enabling administrators graduated from. In fact, I would like to see a study done with the population of convicted teacher sex offenders to identify where they went to college. This data would tell us which colleges are doing a poor job and which are doing a good job and should thus be emulated.

1. Collegiate schools of education need to improve the process of screening and admitting students. For example, several schools could pool their data on graduates who were convicted of sex crimes with students in order to obtain a large sample size. This group of felons could be compared to graduates who were not convicted of sex crimes in order to determine if there are factors that reliably differentiate between the two groups and predict the likelihood of

criminal activity. There may be information in college applications that could be useful in screening out and denying admission to high-probability sexual abusers.

Also, just as I suggest for public schools in the hiring process, collegiate schools of education could work with publishers of psychological tests to develop an instrument to identify individuals with a high probability of sexual abuse. Applicants in this category would be denied admission.

While many schools of education may balk at these recommendations, I would strongly argue that they have a responsibility to society to make every effort to prevent pedophiles from becoming teachers. I firmly believe that parents and the general public would support my position.

2. Collegiate schools of education need to significantly improve their evaluation of mandatory student teaching assignments in order to detect any signs of sexual abuse/harassment. This should include feedback from students, other teachers, and administrators. If the time period allowed for student teaching is too short to allow for an accurate, comprehensive assessment, then it needs to be lengthened.

The bottom line is that collegiate schools of education need to "certify" that their graduates have been rigorously screened and evaluated and are highly unlikely to become sex offenders. Before I would hire a newly graduated teacher, I would want assurances from the college she/he graduated from that every effort had been made to screen out potential child sexual abusers/harassers. Otherwise, why take the chance. Colleges which do take additional steps to prevent this problem will be rewarded in the marketplace with more jobs for their graduates and a better reputation.

3. Collegiate schools of education need to dramatically improve the ways in which they teach students about their professional, moral, and legal responsibilities, with respect to reporting of suspected child sexual abuse/harassment by teachers. While it is illegal not to report suspected abuse, it is also immoral and unprofessional! Not reporting abandons children to continuing trauma and denies them the opportunity for treatment. It is unimaginable that any-

one could do this, much less a teacher who supposedly cares about students.

4. The graduate courses on leadership in education doctoral programs for superintendents need to be redesigned or refocused to emphasize the professional, moral, and legal responsibilities that school administrators have to protect children. "Passing the trash" deals should be unthinkable and out of the question for anyone, especially the superintendent in a school district. Once again, collegiate schools of education need to take responsibility for their role in the pandemic of K-12 student sexual abuse/harassment and aggressively implement corrective strategies.

6. School Accreditation Organizations

Give the extremely high value schools place on being accredited, the organizations responsible for granting accreditation could easily take a leadership role in addressing the pandemic of K-12 student sexual abuse/harassment. For example, if one of the six regional accrediting organizations recognized by the U.S. Department of Education required the reforms I recommended above for school administration, institutions would be compelled to make the necessary changes or face potential denial of accreditation. The rating scale for schools contained in Appendix B or something similar could be used by accrediting bodies to insure that everything possible is being done to prevent and correct the problem of student sexual abuse/harassment.

7. State Teacher Certification Agencies

State agencies that require and process information in order to certify individuals to teach could play a crucial role in addressing the pandemic of K-12 student sexual abuse/harassment. I have four specific recommendations.

First, states could uniformly require all applicants to pass national fingerprint-based criminal background checks to insure that convicted predators are not allowed to teach in any state.

Second, states could seriously consider the use of psychological testing in the certification process to screen out individuals with a high predicted probability of child sexual abuse.

Third, states should uniformly revoke the certification of any teacher who fails to report suspected child abuse.

Fourth, state certification agencies should request additional funding and staff in order to process revocation of certification cases in a more efficient and timely manner. This would insure that offenders lose their certification as quickly as possible and thus also lose their easy access to children.

8. <u>Teachers</u>

I have a great deal to say to teachers and several recommendations that apply to the whole profession, along with specific subsets.

First, let me begin with the microscopic minority of teachers who have in the past and are presently sexually abusing students. <u>You need to stop now!</u> Turn yourself in to police, confess your crimes, and assist in the process of identifying victims so that they can receive professional counseling and support services. Serve your sentence and then find a job in a field that does not involve children. <u>Forever</u>, stay away from our children!

If you don't come forward now, when your crimes are discovered, you will be prosecuted to the fullest extent of the local law. Stop the abuse now and turn yourself in!

Second, I have recommendations for those teachers who have suspected or known about child sexual abuse by a fellow educator and failed to meet their legal, professional, and moral obligations to report it. Your past wrongs need to be corrected now. Any suspected child sexual abuse needs to be immediately reported to the police and school administrators. Assist authorities in trying to identify student victims — those innocent children that you turned your back on — so that they can get professional counseling and support services. Apologize to those children.

Turn yourself in to law enforcement authorities for your failure to report suspected child sexual abuse. Serve your sentence. Try to find an employer willing to hire someone with your record. Vow never to be silent again and enable predators to sexually abuse children.

Third, for those teachers who have never seen or heard of child sexual abuse in their school, never heard of "passing the trash", and never seen the statistics originally published in the Department of Education 2004 report on educator misconduct citing 4.5 million student victims, I recommend that you start paying closer attention to these issues. Your profession is justifiably under assault for the pandemic of K-12 student sexual abuse/harassment and apparent indifference of most teachers.

I am outraged, other parents are outraged, and we expect you to be outraged also, leading the fight to attack this problem There is a lot that needs to be done and I would like to see teachers taking leadership roles in reform initiatives at the classroom, school, district, state, and national levels. We need your help in ridding sexual abuse/harassment from our schools. Please join us!

In addition to reporting suspected child abuse/harassment, I would encourage teachers to: (1) role model appropriate behavior and language for students and colleagues, (2) affirmatively raise the issue of respectful interaction and communication with students, parents, and colleagues, (3) monitor the conduct of your students and colleagues for compliance with the school's sexual abuse/harassment policy, and (4) initiate immediate corrective action if violations occur.

Enlist the Support of an Activist Teacher

Finding an activist teacher within the school system who supports your cause and isn't afraid to stand-up to the administration, the teachers' union, or other teachers can be invaluable. Typically this person should have tenure and thus, some reasonable measure of job security. Otherwise, quick termination by the administration is a likely outcome. While such retaliation for trying to protect student civil rights is illegal, a lengthy lawsuit is often required to get back one's job, plus damages.

In the Jackson v. Birmingham Board of Education case, the Supreme Court ruled in 2005 that school employees can sue school districts for disciplinary action (including wrongful termination) taken against them, as a result of their complaints about discrimination/harassment directed at students.

If you can find a supportive teacher (or teachers, better yet) willing to work with you and other parents to protect students, here are some specific actions that can be implemented.

(1) <u>Classroom Discussion</u> The teacher can include in her/his classes a brief discussion of sexual abuse/sexual harassment, the school policy (if there is one), and how to report complaints.
(2) <u>Classroom Management</u> The teacher can clearly communicate behavioral expectations for classroom conduct, closely monitor classroom interaction, and take immediate steps to correct unacceptable conduct.
(3) <u>Role Model</u> The teacher can role model appropriate professional conduct for all students to see and learn from.
(4) <u>Reporting</u> If student complaints of sexual abuse/harassment are brought to the teacher's attention, she/he should: (a) encourage the student to file a formal complaint with the school and accompany the student to the appropriate office, (b) file his/her own complaint about the reported violation with the school administration, (c) if the reported violation involves potentially criminal conduct, contact both Child Protective Services and local law enforcement authorities, and (d) consider filing an advocate complaint, on behalf of the student, with the Office for Civil Rights of the U.S. Department of Education.
(5) <u>Legal Testimony</u> Perhaps the most potent action available to a teacher is to provide sworn legal testimony in court cases, on behalf of students, whose parents sue the school system, the perpetrator, and/or unresponsive, cowardly administrators over sexual abuse/harassment. Supportive testimony from a teacher against the school district has a powerful impact on judges and juries, and can serve as a strong incentive to schools to settle cases without going to court. Before implementing any of the above strategies, a teacher should carefully consider the following simple questions and answers.

Can the actions discussed above have an immediate impact on the incidence of sexual abuse and sexual harassment at your school? Yes, I have used all of them to effect profound improvements in the sexual harassment climate on the campus where I work and send a powerful message to sexual predators and administrators that the abuse must stop.

Are the recommended pro-student strategies viewed by many in the school community as radical, controversial, and unacceptable? Yes, it is an unfortunate commentary on the values and practices of education that efforts to aggressively protect student civil rights would be viewed with such disdain.

Can you expect that utilizing any of the above strategies will lead to negative consequences for you personally? Yes, you should be prepared to deal with the potential repercussions, including unfavorable faculty committee, union, and administrative decisions, ostracism, lack of collegial support, threats to your personal welfare and that of family members, and frivolous nuisance lawsuits for intimidation purposes.

Can one successfully deal with these negative repercussions? Yes, you learn: (1) to carefully and objectively document your actions and productivity, (2) who your real friends and colleagues are, (3) how to file police reports and take extra safety precautions, and (4) how to file aggressive counter-suits.

Is it all worth it? Yes, when you have talked to as many abuse and harassment victims as I have and seen first-hand the horrible damage that has been inflicted, any efforts on your part to spare another student from this type of suffering are well worth it!

As mentioned earlier, after receiving death threats to my family as a result of my aggressive, pro-student actions on campus in the late 1990's, I was forced to relocate to another state, 100 miles away. This provided a much-needed sense of safety and security to the entire family. Luckily, since 1999, we have not had any incidents.

I will repeat the quote cited earlier in the book by Edmund Burke: "All that is necessary for the triumph of evil is that good men [and women] do nothing." Teachers need to become part of the solution, not part of the problem. Good luck finding a strong teacher to support your efforts to protect children!

CONCLUSIONS

The pandemic of K-12 student sexual abuse/harassment plaguing U.S. schools has multiple powerful causes that are firmly entrenched in our society. Effectively attacking these causes will be neither quick nor easy. Success requires a concerted effort over time by parents and concerned citizens.

There are many potent strategies that individual parents can implement to substantially improve protection of our children in school. I encourage you to try out different corrective approaches and experiment with new ones. The more of us who get involved and take action, the quicker we will prevail. Good luck in your fight, and remember that child safety and welfare have to be our top priority!

APPENDIX A

SELECTED REFERENCES AND RESOURCES

AAUW Educational Foundation (2001) Hostile Hallways: Bullying, Teasing, and Sexual Harassment in School. Washington, D.C.

AAUW Educational Foundation (2004) Harassment-Free Hallways. Washington, D.C.

AAUW Educational Foundation (2011) Crossing the Line: Sexual Harassment at School. Washington, D.C.

Abel, G.G. & Harlow, N. (2001) Stop Child Molestation. Xlibris Corporation

American Association of School Administrators, www.aasa.org

American Civil Liberties Union. Gender-Based Violence and Harassment: Your School, Your Rights. www.aclu.org/files/assets/genderbasedviolence_factsheet_0.pdf
The Association of Missing & Exploited Children Organizations (AMECO), www.amecoinc.org

Canadian Centre for Child Protection, Kids in the Know, www.kidsintheknow.ca

Cannon v. U. of Chicago, Supreme Court Case (1979)

Child Abuse Forensic Institute, www.childabuseforensics.org

Creating Safer Havens, http://creatingsaferhavens.com

Davis v. Monroe County Board of Education, Supreme Court Case (1999)

Eckes, S. (2006) Reducing Peer Sexual Harassment in Schools. <u>Education Digest</u>, 71, 7, 36-40

Fitzgerald v. Barnstable School Committee, Supreme Court Case (2009)

Franklin v. Gwinnett County Public Schools, Supreme Court Case (1992)

Gebser v. Lago Independent School District, Supreme Court Case (1998)

George, S.J. (2010) So Sexual Harassment Plaintiffs Get Two Bites of the Apple?: Sexual Harassment Litigation After Fitzgerald v. Barnstable School Committee, <u>Drake Law Review</u>, 59, 41, p. 1-21

Goldstein, S. (1999) <u>The Sexual Exploitation of Children</u>. CRC Press: Boca Raton, FL

Goss-Graves, F. (2011) On Federal Enforcement of Civil Rights Laws to Protect Students Against Bullying, Violence, and Harassment. Testimony to the U.S. Commission on Civil Rights, May 13, 2011, Washington, D.C.: National Women's Law Center

Hobson, C.J. & Hobson, C. (2002) <u>The Lecherous University: What Every Student & Parent Should Know About the Epidemic of Sexual Harassment on Campus</u>. Bangor, ME: Booklocker.com

Jackson v. Birmingham Board of Education, Supreme Court Case (2005)

Meyer, E.J. (2008) Gendered Harassment in Secondary Schools: Understanding Teachers' (Non)Interventions. Gender and Education, 20, 6, p. 555-70

Meyouhas, T. (2010) Eleventh Annual Review of Gender and Sexuality Law: Educational Law Chapter: Sexual Harassment in Education, The Georgetown Journal of Gender and the Law, 11, 297, p. 1-20

National Center for Missing and Exploited Children, www.missingkids.com

The National Center for Victims of Crime, www.victimsofcrime.org

The National Child Traumatic Stress Network, www.nctsn.org

National Coalition of Women and Girls in Education (2008) Title IX at 35: Beyond the Headlines. Washington, D.C.

The National Crime Victim Bar Association, www.victimbar.org

National Women's Law Center, www.nwlc.org

Office for Civil Rights (1992) Nondiscrimination on the Basis of Sex in Education Programs and Activities Receiving or Benefiting from Federal Financial Assistance

Office for Civil Rights (1997) Sexual Harassment Guidance: Harassment of Students by School Employees, Other Students or Third Parties, revised, 2001

Office for Civil Rights (2006) Dear Colleague Letter, Sexual Harassment Issues

Office for Civil Rights (2008) Sexual Harassment: It's Not Academic (revised)

Office for Civil Rights (2010) Case Processing Manual (CPM) (revised)

Office for Civil Rights (2010) Dear Colleague Letter, Guidance on Civil Rights Responsibility for Bullying and Harassment

Office for Civil Rights (2011) Dear Colleague Letter, Sexual Violence Guidance

Ormerod, A.J., Collinsworth, L.L., & Perry, L.A. (2008) Critical Climate: Relations among Sexual Harassment, Climate, and Outcomes for High School Girls and Boys. Psychology of Women Quarterly, 32, 2, p. 113-25.

Rubin, S. & Biggs, J.S. (1999) Teachers That [Who] Sexually Abuse Students. Lancaster, PA: Technomic Publishing Co., Inc.

Sandler, B.R. & Stonehill, H.M. (2005) Student-to-Student Sexual Harassment K-12: Strategies and Solutions for Educators to Use in the Classroom, School, and Community. Lanham, MD: Rowman & Littlefield

Sang Walker, G. (2010) The Evolution and Limits of Title IX Doctrine on Peer Sexual Assault, Harvard Civil Rights – Civil Liberties Law Review, 45, 95, p. 1-34

Shakeshaft, C. (2003) Educator Sexual Abuse, Hofstra Horizons, Spring, p. 10-13

Stein, N. & Mennemeier, K.A. (2011) Sexual Harassment Overview: Concerns, New Directions, and Strategies. In National Summit on Gender-Based Violence Among Young People reading materials (p. 1-28) www2.ed.gov/about/offices/list/osdfs/gbvreading.pdf

Stop Educator Sexual Abuse, Misconduct and Exploitation (S.E.S.A.M.E.), www.sesamenet.org

Teachertenure.procon.org

Thompson Publishing Group (2012) Educator's Guide to Controlling Sexual Harassment. Washington, D.C.

U.S. Department of Education, Office of the Under Secretary (2004) Educator Sexual Misconduct: A Synthesis of Existing Literature, Washington, D.C.

U.S. Department of Education (February 22, 2012) Response to Freedom of Information Act Request No. 12-00353-F

U.S. Government Accountability Office (2010) Report to the Chairman, Committee on Education and Labor, House of Representatives. K-12 Education: Selected Cases of Public and Private Schools That Hired or Retained Individuals with Histories of Sexual Misconduct

Yello Dyno, Inc., www.yellodyno.com

Young, A.M., Grey, M., & Boyd, C.J. (2008) Adolescents' Experiences of Sexual Assault by Peers: Prevalence and Nature of Victimization Occurring Within and Outside of School. Journal of Youth and Adolescence, 38, 8, p. 1072-83.

PASSING THE TRASH

APPENDIX B

SCHOOL SEXUAL ABUSE/HARASSMENT PREVENTION RATING SCALE©

AN ASSESSMENT GUIDE FOR PARENTS, TEACHERS, AND ADMINISTRATORS

SCHOOL SEXUAL ABUSE/HARASSMENT PREVENTION RATING SCALE©

1. <u>Formal School Policies Related to Sexual Abuse/Harassment</u> (15 possible points)

    _____(1 pt.)   1.   The school has a written zero-tolerance policy prohibiting sexual abuse/harassment of students.

    _____(1 pt.)   2.   The school has a policy prohibiting employees from being alone with students.

    _____(1 pt.)   3.   The school has a strict policy concerning employees touching students.

    _____(1 pt.)   4.   The school has a designated Title IX Coordinator and a contact person in every building.

    _____(1 pt.)   5.   Information about the school sexual abuse/harassment policy and Title IX Coordinator is widely and periodically disseminated to students and parents.

_____ (1 pt.)   6.   All school employees and administrators are required to report any incident of suspected child sexual abuse to law enforcement.

_____ (1 pt.)   7.   All school employees are required to report any suspected sexual abuse/harassment to the administration.

_____ (2 pts.)   8.   Thorough fingerprint-based national criminal background checks are conducted on all applicants for school employment.

_____ (2 pts.)   9.   Applicants for employment must sign liability waivers allowing former employers to give complete references.

_____ (1 pt.)   10.   Applicants for employment must provide written and signed responses to questions about prior sexual misconduct involving students.

_____ (1 pt.)   11.   Thorough, fingerprint-based national criminal background checks are conducted on all prospective school volunteers.

_____(1 pt.)   12.   Letters of reference for employees who resign while under investigation for sexual abuse/harassment clearly indicate this fact.

_____(1 pt.)   13.   A written student survey of school sexual harassment is conducted annually.

_____ Sub-Total Points

(also enter in the appropriate box on the scoring summary sheet – last page).

2. <u>Sexual Abuse/Harassment Training</u>
(10 possible points)

    _____(3 pts.)   1.   <u>Mandatory</u> annual sexual abuse/harassment training for <u>all</u> teachers and school employees.

    _____(3 pts.)   2.   <u>Mandatory</u> annual sexual abuse/harassment training for <u>all</u> students.

    _____(1 pt.)   3.   <u>Mandatory</u> annual additional training for school administrators on their roles and responsibilities.

    _____(1 pt.)   4.   <u>Mandatory</u> sexual abuse/harassment training for <u>all</u> substitute teachers and school volunteers.

    _____(2 pts.)   5.   Sexual abuse/harassment training workshops available for parents.

_____ Sub-Total Points

(also enter in the appropriate box on the
scoring summary sheet – last page)

3. <u>Student Support Services</u> (5 possible points)

    _____(1 pt.)   1.   24-hour crisis hotline is available for student use.

    _____(4 pts.)   2.   Free professional counseling services are available to students who have been sexually abused/harassed and their families.

_____ Sub-Total Points

(also enter in the appropriate box on the scoring summary sheet – last page).

4. <u>Complaint Processing and Investigations</u>
   (20 possible points)

   _____(2 pts.)   1. Multiple complaint filing options are available to students and parents, including any teacher or administrator and anonymous phone or web-based systems.

   _____(2 pts.)   2. If appropriate, the complainant is immediately referred for counseling.

   _____(2 pts.)   3. The complainant and alleged abuser/harasser are immediately separated at school, pending results of an investigation.

   _____(2 pts.)   4. Documented periodic monitoring of the complainant is conducted to insure that the alleged harassment has stopped and no retaliation has occurred.

   _____(1 pt.)   5. If retaliation is documented, immediate corrective action is initiated.

   _____(2 pts.)   6. <u>All</u> complaints are investigated.

   _____(2 pts.)   7. Investigations are conducted by <u>independent</u>, <u>professionally-qualified</u> personnel.

_____(1 pt.)   8.   A central record is maintained of all complaints and resolution outcomes.

_____(2 pts.)   9.   For complaints alleging flagrant/criminal violations, the school employee involved is suspended with pay from all student-contact activities, pending the results of a thorough investigation.

_____(2 pts.)   10.   If an investigation produces evidence of a possible criminal violation, the case is also submitted to the local prosecutor's office.

_____(1 pt.)   11.   Students who initiate a complaint with the school are informed about <u>all</u> of their filing options, including the OCR and law enforcement agencies.

_____(1 pt.)   12.   When evaluating a complaint filed against a particular individual, all previous complaints and disciplinary actions are fully reviewed.

_____ Sub-Total Points

(also enter in the appropriate box on the scoring summary sheet – last page).

6. <u>Discipline</u> (25 possible points)

_____(8 pts.) 1. Documented abusers/harassers are strongly disciplined (including <u>for employees</u>—suspension without pay, permanent cessation of all student-contact activities, mandatory counseling, supervised interaction with students, termination); <u>for students</u>—mandatory counseling, suspension, expulsion.

_____(8 pts.) 2. For repeated and/or flagrant documented incidents of sexual abuse/harassment, school employees are terminated, students are permanently expelled.

_____(4 pts.) 3. School employees who fail to report suspected sexual abuse/harassment are strongly disciplined, up to and including termination.

_____(1 pt.) 4. School employees who fail to attend mandatory sexual abuse/harassment training are formally disciplined.

_____(2 pts.) 5. School employees are disciplined for violations of the policy prohibiting being alone with students.

_____(2 pts.) 6. School employees are disciplined for violations of the student touching policy.

_____ Sub-Total Points

(also enter in the appropriate box on the scoring summary sheet – last page).

7. <u>Public Reporting and Information Dissemination</u>
   (25 possible points)

   _____(10 pts.)   1.   Summary statistics on the incidence of school sexual abuse/harassment are published annually, posted to the school website, and provided to current/ prospective students and their parents.

   _____(5 pts.)   2.   Summaries of individual sexual abuse/harassment complaints (to include: charges, findings, and actions taken, but no names of the persons involved) are published annually, posted to the school website, and provided to current/prospective students and their parents.

   _____(4 pts.)   3.   Results of the annual student sexual abuse/harassment survey are published at the school website and provided to current/prospective students and their parents.

   _____(3 pts.)   4.   Information about how to use the school's sexual abuse/harassment complaint processing system and other filing options is emailed/mailed annually

_____ (3 pts.)   5.   to all students and their parents.

Information about school sexual abuse/harassment, complaint procedures and filing options is publicly and prominently posted in all school buildings.

_____ Sub-Total Points

(also enter in the appropriate box on the scoring summary sheet – last page).

©2012, C. J. Hobson

SCHOOL SEXUAL ABUSE/HARASSMENT

PREVENTION RATING SCALE©

Scoring Summary Sheet

_____ 1. Formal School Policies (15 possible points)

_____ 2. Sexual Abuse/Harassment Training
(10 possible points)

_____ 3. Student Support Services (5 possible points)

_____ 4. Complaint Processing and Investigations
(20 possible points)

_____ 5. Discipline (25 possible points)

_____ 6. Public Reporting and Information Dissemination
(25 possible points)

_____ Total (100 possible points)

©2012, C. J. Hobson

APPENDIX C

ABOUT THE AUTHOR

Charles J. Hobson earned his Ph.D. in Industrial/Organizational Psychology from Purdue in 1981. He is currently a Professor of Management at Indiana University Northwest. Dr. Hobson has 31 years of experience teaching undergraduate and M.B.A. courses in organizational behavior and human resource management. He has served as a consultant and trainer to 172 companies and universities, including several Fortune 500 firms, and functioned as an expert witness in 39 employment and education discrimination cases, often involving sexual abuse/harassment allegations. Dr. Hobson has 147 professional publications/presentations and two books, including multiple articles on academic and workplace sexual harassment.

Made in the USA
Lexington, KY
05 February 2018